Information in Action

Soft Systems Methodology

GW00535658

MACMILLAN INFORMATION SYSTEMS SERIES

Series Editor: Professor I. O. Angell

Information in Action
Soft Systems Methodology
Lynda Davies and Paul Ledington

Information Systems Management
Opportunities and Risks
Ian O. Angell and Steve Smithson

Understanding Information
An Introduction
Jonathan Leibenau and James Backhouse

Developing Information Systems
Concepts, Issues and Practice
Christianthi Avgeron and Tony Cornford

Computer Security Within Organizations
Adrian R. Warman

Information in Action

Soft Systems Methodology

Lynda Davies

Griffith University
Australia

Paul Ledington

University of Queensland
Australia

MACMILLAN

First published 1991 by
THE MACMILLAN PRESS LTD
Houndmills, Basingstoke, Hampshire RG21 2XS
and London
Companies and representatives
throughout the world

ISBN 0–333–56539–8

A catalogue record for this book is available
from the British Library.

Printed in China

Reprinted 1993

Dedicated to

Peter Stewart Walsh

and

David James Walsh

Contents

Preface   viii

Diagramming conventions   xi

Acknowledgements   xiii

1. Introduction   1

Part I. The learning process of soft systems methodology   9

2. Soft systems methodology: an illustrative study   10

3. Problem situations   30

Part II. Soft systems modelling   57

4. Modelling human activity systems: root definitions of relevant systems   58

5. Modelling human activity systems: generating models   84

6. Comparison   105

Part III. Reflections   132

7. Using the methodology   133

8. Reflecting on the learning process   158

Index   165

Preface

This book is intended primarily for students of the management of information. It is unlikely that this will place the book in any set discipline but rather should find it of use across a variety of courses. This variety is likely to include information systems specialists as well as those involved with management courses which treat information as a fundamental attribute of managerial life. The term 'student' is being used in its broadest sense as anyone seeking to learn about a topic, whether on a formal course or not. However, the aim has been to make this a textbook so that it should fit easily into semester courses, though it also supports shorter courses or even postgraduate courses of longer duration.

The primary purpose of the book is to enhance learning. This means that references and citations have been minimalized to the point of almost total exclusion. Instead, suggested readings are given at the end of each chapter or section. This should help those who wish to follow the ideas further. The learning is also enhanced by the inclusion of discussion issues and exercises at the end of each chapter. A further enhancement is in the way that an illustrative study is given at the beginning of the book and then reflected upon in later chapters.

This book explores a fundamentally different view of information from that presented in the majority of information systems texts. This view is that information is continually being created in social life as we try to make sense of our worlds. Learning and information are mutually dependent in this process. Managing information is a process which we do all the time in ordering and renegotiating our realities. The process of managing creates information, which in turn creates a process of managing. It is usually implicit and intuitive and this creates problems for us when we have to socially negotiate our meanings. We misunderstand because we cannot easily make explicit what the issues are with which we are struggling. In exploring this vision of managing information, we realize that more formal processes are needed for helping the sense-making process to become ordered and explicit. One such process is in the form of a methodology which adopts a view of social reality creation and management that is highly compatible with our views on managing information. This is soft systems methodology. We take readers through that methodology so that they can learn it in order to apply it to the managing of information as a learning process.

The **Introduction** challenges current views of information management by arguing that management is a learning process which we carry out all the time. The main problem is that we need to make the process more explicit so that we can better understand what is going on. In this way, information management becomes the management of the learning process and soft systems methodology is introduced as an approach for helping that learning process. The role of information technology is also discussed.

In Part I, we look at **The learning process of soft systems methodology** and work through this by looking at an illustrative study which is an account of one author's use of the methodology. This provides the initial understanding of the methodology which is then looked at in greater depth as the concept of **Problem situations** is introduced. It is here that we look at culture, politics, roles of intervenors, and the notion of problems as social attributes created in a social world of sense-making. This sets the context of an understanding of social reality that is fundamental both to soft systems methodology and to the explanation of managing information which the book presents. In this section the story of an intervention using soft systems methodology is unfolded. It is treated in a personalized manner as is commonplace in accounts of interventions using a phenomenological view of the social sciences. This is the view adopted throughout the book but which is most obvious in this section.

Part II moves onto the technical aspects of carrying out the methodology in a rigorous and defensible manner. It is here that **Soft systems modelling** is concentrated on. The fundamental concept of a soft systems model is that of the human activity system. This is generated through two technical operations which are presented in detail in the chapters **Modelling human activity systems: root definitions of relevant systems** and **Modelling human activity systems: generating models**. Relevant systems are chosen, that is, ideal type systems which are relevant to learning about the problem situation. These are then developed into core descriptions which are called root definitions. These each express a particular world view. The descriptions are then translated into models of human activity systems which represent the actions expressed in the root definitions. This means that the activities associated with the different world views can be understood and this provides the groundwork for the next stage, namely **Comparison** of the models with the real world problem situation. Comparison is the most powerful part of the methodology, as it is here that learning occurs in the process of gaining clarity regarding the different views in the situation.

Part III deals with **Reflections**. Here the learning which has hopefully occurred throughout the reading of the book is challenged and developed. The first way in which this is done is to return to the illustrative study, revisiting it by looking at the reality of **Using the methodology**. It is too easy to believe that a methodology will bring about answers all by itself. It cannot, and this is discussed in the chapter. Every situation has different issues and this should cause reflection on the part of the practitioner, who is trying to make sense of the situation and to help those within it to understand what is happening and what can be done. This chapter tells the 'warts-and-all' version of a particular intervention. The aim is to provide an experiential account which may help naive users to avoid the painful process of expecting too much of a methodology, and so avoid the likelihood of being let down as a result. The chapter aims to help by highlighting the fact that often the situations which are read about will have had traumatic problems, but all recording of these will normally have been removed. Academic authorship in learned journals regularly requires this depersonalization. However, learning can come from these traumas and so they are worthy of attention. It helps the discovery process to see what actual problem situations can be like. It also prevents the feeling of failure, which may not be justified. Getting into difficulties is not necessarily a failure and this is discussed in a somewhat reflective manner. The final chapter takes a stance of **Reflecting on the learning process**. This leads the reader back to arguments given in the introduction and revisits the view of managing information given there, expanding upon it. The manager of information acting as a guide for the learning process is the central theme of the chapter. The methodology is reflected upon in the light of this, as the different sections of the book are briefly revisited. Whilst reflection is the theme of this section, it is the notion of managing information which is the main argument of this book and the book concludes by re-examining this.

Information systems as a discipline is a hybrid which is attached to many other disciplines. This is probably not a bad thing. Information is central to our lives, therefore we cannot avoid it. We can choose to study it in expressed forms and through particular frameworks but we cannot pinpoint it down to a set area of study, or at least attempting to do so may be futile, if not potentially destructive. Taking the management of information seriously as a continual daily social process is central to our message. Soft systems methodology is a framework for enhancing that process by improving learning. We hope that this book helps the reader to understand that message and to improve the creation and management of information as a result of the learning process.

Diagramming conventions

In soft systems methodology there is a heavy reliance upon diagramming as a means of expression and communication. The diagramming has some formal conventions and some informal. The use of diagrams is also a major element in the general field of information systems modelling, but there the conventions are very much different from those of soft systems methodology. In order to prevent any confusion, the conventions for all diagram types in soft systems methodology that are used in this book are given below:

Rich Pictures

The purpose of rich pictures (e.g. figure 2.3) is to provide an *aide-mémoire* for gaining an appreciation of the problem situation. Rich pictures are of the form of free artistic expression, and are intrinsically individualistic in their expressive style. Basically, there are no conventions of diagramming, except one, and that is that no systems models or systems maps are used at the rich picture stage. All arrows and boxes are merely artistic expressions – they are not, repeat not, conventional forms.

Diagrams

These are used as an explanation in pictorial form of the flow of an argument. They are not models of systems as such. Diagrams of the summary description of the methodology (e.g. figure 2.1) are of this form. They simply present the written text as a series of statements which flow in the form of a logical argument. An arrow means "leads to", and a box, polygon or oval means "a descriptive statement".

Conceptual models

It is in this type of diagram (e.g. figure 5.6) that the formal conventions of soft systems modelling apply. All the aspects of a conceptual model are rule-based and meaningful in conventional terms. The thinner arrows mean "logical relationships", thicker arrows mean "commodity inputs and outputs". Boxes, polygons and ovals mean "activities". When more than one activity is boxed together then this box represents a sub-system. Zig-zag arrows show a logical relationship to, or from, all parts of the system.

Acknowledgements

This book is the result of a continual learning process, lasting around a decade, that has engrossed the authors. The wider learning context has been going on for over twenty years at the Department of Systems and Information Management at Lancaster University, U.K. We are extremely grateful to the members of that department for the creation of a learning context and for providing the means whereby we could flourish in our associative learning with them. Peter Checkland is a key member of that department and did much more than simply provide learning. He and Glen Checkland have provided valuable friendship, which has led to many of the reflections making this book possible.

We are also grateful to our soft systems community around the world who have been part of the clarification process needed for this book to happen. The other primary player is the cheery-natured Welshman whose intellectual residence is LSE. Ian Angell contrived this book out of us and for this we are very grateful. We are also grateful to Griffith University and the University of Queensland for providing the necessary support and to the many students who have challenged us and helped us along the way. Special thanks also go to our colleagues and friends Tim Davis and Sue Nielsen.

Finally, we want to acknowledge the debt owed to our family. We have only one combined family as we are in the unusual position of being joint working spouses. Thanks, Mum, David and Peter. And Lynda says 'thank you' to her husband Paul, the same as Paul says 'thank you' to his wife Lynda.

1 Introduction

- *Challenging the hidden assumptions*
- *Managing the learning process*
- *The role of information technology*
- *Information management*

Managing information is something we do all our lives. It is possibly because we do it so often that we do not reflect on what exactly it is. Life is already complicated enough and so overcomplicating it with unnecessary self-reflection is something we inherently avoid. That is all well and good, always provided that we are not accountable for our actions, or are not actively involved in assessing these actions to evaluate possible changes. Most of the time intuitive action is enough. However, there are times when we need more than this, and that is when accountable frameworks, which can stand the criticism of enquiry, are needed. Currently it seems that many models of information management are being used without that critical enquiry, and some rather limiting models of both information and its management are dominating our thoughts and actions.

This book is one of a series that challenges those models in an informative and helpful way. Liebenau and Backhouse (1990) start that challenge by presenting the fundamental argument that information and computers are being inadvertently equated. Computers may be useful tools for handling data bits which can be used as information, but those data bits are not information *per se*. Also, computers and software may be designed to manage those bits but they do not do the managing. It is the designers and the users who deal with that end of the spectrum. Computers are handy, but dumb. They are potential supporters for the management of information, but they cannot take on the act of information management itself. Therefore, the equating of computers with the management of information has to be challenged, in order that a better understanding of both information and its management can emerge.

Challenging the hidden assumptions

Information is often assumed to be the same as data. It is not. Information is concerned with interpretation, that is, somebody has started to make sense of something. As an example, we shall look at traffic lights as information. Traffic lights are merely physical objects with a sequence of rules operating light shifts. Even so, they are potent social controllers, telling many millions of drivers what to do if they wish to drive safely and so avoid prosecution or worse. It is in their use that they become informative. The designers of the traffic light had to come up with a technical design which was technically feasible under many different environmental conditions, economically possible to install in many different economic states, had enough differentiation in signals to allow for clarity of message, yet simplistic enough to avoid irrelevant ambiguity and to minimize possible misinterpretations. The traffic light was an output from a consideration of a multitude of related problem areas. It had to provide explicit information across many nations and decades. It is an exemplary type of information management action, dealing with a multitude of constraints and issues by applying rigour and simplicity. At the time of its initial development, it had nothing to do with computers and handled the management of information superbly.

This is just one example of the management of information which is not necessarily computer based. Looking at the process by which the information could have been managed to end up with the traffic light design is enlightening when we think of information and its management. First, there was a complex and highly integrated area of concern which was that of signalling to road users how to behave when approaching junctions which have a heavy flow of through traffic. Although explicit rules in the form of highway codes have been devised, these are still partially ambiguous and leave decisions on how to act up to the judgement of individuals. The recognition had to be made that more formal and explicit rules for action were required where ambiguity of judgement and action could be excluded. This is a comparatively easy exercise once we know what we are looking for, that is, once the design solution has been dreamed up, implemented and generally known to be highly effective under the majority of circumstances. It is much more difficult, though, when the issue is just a feeling of needing to do something about the situation. What it is about the situation that enables design alternatives to occur is likely to be uncertain at first. What are going to be selected as relevant issues and important points to consider have to be learned about. The information required for that learning will not be obvious but will become more so as the process of discovery unfolds.

Some approaches to the analysis of information requirements do not necessarily recognize that the nomination of relevant requirements is a learning process. These approaches act as if the problem is only technical, and a well-structured, mechanistic approach to tackling the problem is all that is required. Those who have dealt with information analysis know that this is folly. Understanding requirements means getting involved in the learning process and actively asking what is informative and what is not as the learning emerges. Information becomes emergent as the problem areas are delved into and possible ways of handling them are approached. Information management becomes a process of learning, with management becoming an orchestration process rather than a goal-directed move down an explicit path.

This shows not only that information management is not simply equatable with computers, but also that it is not just a series of technically devised steps which will move to an easily identifiable solution. Instead, once the fundamental area of concern has been identified then so will the associated information, and the management procedures will have enfolded as part of the design process chosen for dealing with the area of concern. The really difficult part is identifying the area of concern in a way that can be openly discussed with the necessary degree of clarity. Understanding the situation must come first, so that what is information in that situation can be understood and the appropriate and acceptable management processes related to that information can be adopted. From the above example, once the control of drivers' behaviour under certain circumstances was recognized as being of primary concern, the recognition of visual signals as being informative, sequences to be even more informative, and lights to run the sequences as being an effective way of managing that information was relatively easy. Once the concerns are made explicit and can be debated, then managing information becomes a much more simple and obvious process.

Managing the learning process

Information management is about managing a learning process. This allows for designs to unfold which can then be the basis of further information management. This occurs as users of the resultant design for information management then take part in a related learning process, which in turn allows for further interpretation, further learning, and so on. This moves away from the view that information exists as some object in the world, and that we can capture, store, manipulate and retrieve it. Instead we query, learn, challenge and change by continually reconstructing what is informative in relation to our learning actions. Information is then treated as part of a learning process rather than as an object. The management of information then becomes the management of the learning process. In this second view information and discovery are more correctly equated than are information and data.

To illustrate the difference, imagine the world of a young infant. If the world was of structured information objects which demanded capturing, then the infant would have to be pre-determined to recognize the information objects. The recognition would be followed by cutting out the object from the rest of the world and taking it, that is, capturing it. A representation of the information object would be stored, presumably in the infant's head, as a piece of information. It would then be retrieved at a later date. Nowhere in this process would it change form. Interpretation would not be required, only recognition of the object. The information would not have to be meaningful in any other way. The infant would be a passive processor, acting mainly as a store for the information objects.

An alternative world of the infant is one where learning occurs through discovery. The world is full of potential information and the selection of what is informative and what is not is done by constructing cognitive frameworks of the world of which questions are asked so that sense can be made of the world. What is informative is continually being reinterpreted according to the queries being asked of the world. The process is curiosity-driven and the object of the exercise is to learn and develop, not just to store. The process is active and information is dependent upon interpretation. Information has meaning according to the interpretation which is happening, and the infant is an active discoverer in the information management process known as learning. This is a view of information only being real when it is associated with action that is interpretation.

Most approaches to information analysis deal with the first model or view of the world, mentioned above. This book has a view of information and its management which is related to the second model. This means that the management of the learning process is fundamental to the management of information. It is through this learning process that the questioning of the world becomes ordered as acts of appreciation, demanding interpretation and constant relearning. Information and enquiry are locked together through a process of interpretation.

The role of information technology

Information technology comes in many forms. To simplify matters, only computer-based information technology is being considered here. This form of technology is both a tool for supporting the learning process and an artifact which has information value itself. Computers as tools allow for large-scale actions regarding information usage to occur. Many people in diverse geographical settings can communicate instantly. Many pieces of data can be simultaneously, or sequentially, processed to support the learning process, and they can be stored to aid in future learning processes. Computer operations can become an extension of the computational operations of the mind. However, they do not replace the interpretive operations but rather provide support for those operations. Computers are very good at data-handling, which can then be used as information support in the learning process of information management.

Computers as artifacts refers to the understanding of technology as social constructions. People can like or dislike computers, find them useful, irritating, productive, destructive, functional or intrusive, for example. These value-stances interpret computers as certain forms of technology. They attribute values to the technology and in so doing often attribute them with many other characteristics. They make them meaningful objects in their social world of work. This has very little connection with what computers do as data processors, and has far more to do with how they are interpreted as artifacts. They can be attributed with personalities or idiosyncrasies and strange ritualistic behaviour can be attached to them. For example, there have been instances of people refusing to operate computers unless they can first tap them, knock them, or switch them on in particular sequences which are not necessarily required technically. People build mental models of them as having a will of their own, and the fear of the computers applying that will against the will of the user leads to ritualized behaviour. What appear to be magical dance sequences are performed and the machines are chanted at in such manners as "Now you behave yourself" or "Hello, machine, I hope you are feeling good today." Users talk of having to discuss procedures with their machines before using them, setting up some form of negotiated contract between themselves and their machines. They build up whole worlds in which the machines are meaningful contributors to that world. They sometimes even give them names, putting labels or pictures onto them, or into them. The machines become a form of totem pole for the worship of the technology as part of the working life which is daily reconstructed. In this sense, the machine as an object itself becomes attributed with meaning. It is an artifact, without actually having to do anything functional at all! Its function is separated from its interpretation and it becomes a symbol of communicated interaction, rather than just a storer and processor of data. Computers often 'live' in organizational worlds in this manner.

Information management

Managing information is managing the learning process of discovery. That can happen in an intuitive manner but sometimes it needs to be handled in a more explicit form. Computers can support this process but they do not equate with the process. A further support comes in the form of a more formal and explicit framework for understanding the learning process. This is a methodology which has emerged through action as a way of understanding the learning process. This understanding allows for learning to be appreciated, clarified, monitored, and reconstructed as necessary. It acts as a means of managing the process of learning known as information management.

The methodology presented in this book is soft systems methodology (SSM) which has emerged as a way of orchestrating the debate of the learning process. It is a way of managing the process of managing information. It is primarily of use in helping people in ill-understood situations to understand the information that they are trying to manage. It helps to identify the information process by identifying the interpretations of the situation. It helps with the analysis of information in a situation but also with understanding and managing of the process of design. At the core of SSM is the concept of the human activity system. This is the understanding of human actions as sense-making actions which can be treated as systemic forms for the purpose of asking questions about them. These actions are interpretations and so both use information and create information. It is actions which provide the basis for interpretations and through this that sense is made of the world.

Soft systems methodology formalizes the process whereby we learn about the world. It is a framework for understanding the world as different perspectives, with different attributes and different artifacts attached to them. It is a framework which can be used to guide learning, and so used to guide the understanding of information and its management. Once this has occurred the more formal and structured data analysis can follow so that computers can store and process the learning outputs in data forms. The methodology allows for learning to be understood as information so that the information can later be constructed as data for processing by computers. The learning is the fundamental starting point in this process and making the learning explicit is the first step in understanding the related information. The continuing learning process then needs further managing as the process of information interpretation and management is revisited.

Soft systems methodology is unfolded in this book. It is done for the purposes of creating a learning process. Technical operations are presented along with a more discursive background to these operations. The learning process should lead to a richer understanding of information and its management than that of the structuring of data for computer processing and storage. The management of learning is central to human action, which must be information-based or otherwise sense-making could not occur.

This view of managing information is unashamedly human-centred and considers as fundamental the understanding of organizational life as a process of sense-making. People create information. They manage it through interpretation. It is people that we need to understand when dealing with information management. If we do that then we can better understand the role of information technology in the management of information.

Discussion issues

1. Consider how information is managed when television news is programmed and delivered. How are different interpretations of the events presented and how are the viewers guided towards their interpretations?

2. Discuss whether a diary is informative or not. What do you think are the fundamental things that are needed to make a diary informative? What is more acceptable as data in a diary?

3. Discuss how learning to drive may be viewed as information management.

Suggested reading

Checkland, P.B., *Systems thinking, systems practice,* Wiley, Chichester, 1981.
    The original work on soft systems methodology.

Checkland, P.B. & Scholes, J., *Soft systems methodology in action,* Wiley, Chichester, 1990.
    An update to the 1981 book which also gives greater consideration to aspects of using the methodology.

Hirschheim, R.A., *Office automation: a social and organizational perspective,* Wiley, Chichester, 1984.
    A useful book for looking at different methodologies and how they relate to the notion of information as interpretation.

Liebenau, J. & Backhouse, J., *Understanding information: an introduction,* Macmillan Information Systems Series, Macmillan, London, 1990.
    Some very fruitful discussions of what is information are to be found in this book.

Wilson, B., *Systems: Concepts, methodologies, and applications,* Wiley, Chichester, 1984.
    This links soft systems methodology to the analysis of information processes through the development of information systems methodology. It is a useful addition to the Checkland writings.

Part I

The learning process of soft systems methodology

In the following two chapters, we look at the context in which the methodology is applied. The first chapter presents an overview of the methodology in the form of an illustrative study. This is so that the reader can get a taste for the methodology before learning its more technical aspects. This chapter also provides the basis for reflection at the end of the book and acts a source of material for later exercises. The second chapter introduces the reader to the initial analytical forms used in soft systems methodology. These are all concerned with analysis of the social world known as the problem situation. The analyses look at roles, culture, and politics in some detail.

This section deals with the social world in which the methodology is developed and applied. Understanding that social world is fundamental to understanding the methodology as a learning process which is enhanced by the use of systems thinking. The section presents the groundwork for the modelling technicalities presented in Part II.

2 Soft systems methodology: An illustrative study

- *Soft systems methodology*
- *The illustrative study*
- *Analysis of the problem situation*
- *Representation of the problem situation*
- *The development of the systems thinking*
- *Comparison and action*

The opening chapter presented soft systems methodology as an approach to managing information. This section of the book introduces the methodology. In essence, the whole book expands soft systems methodology, and this chapter gives a first view of it. This means that the reader can get a general understanding of it before journeying into the detail that the rest of the book provides. Throughout the book a version of the methodology is followed which is the most commonly known. This is the version of the methodology seen as a seven-stage model, as is shown in figure 2.1, below. This version is merely a metaphor to describe a complex set of actions which is called soft systems methodology. That metaphor is an ideal type in that it is not the way any real world use of the methodology is likely to look, but rather it is a model to provide guidelines for action. This distinction between the methodology in principle and the methodology in practice is discussed throughout this book, but most fully in chapter 7.

Soft systems methodology

The seven-stage model shows that the methodology makes a distinction between activities which are related directly to the real world of the problem situation and activities which relate to the world of systems thinking. This is not a trivial separation. All of the methodology is conducted on real world problem situations when it is used, but the principles for the methodology state that certain real world aspects have to be considered as separate from certain systems thinking aspects. The whole of the methodology is a systemic form in that the model as a whole represents a systems view of idealized action. This means that soft systems methodology is a systemic process which uses systems thinking, that is, it is doubly systemic. The relevance of this will become more apparent towards the end of the book. The key reason for separating the aspects dealing with the real world from aspects dealing with systems thinking is so that the real world development of systems models are not confused. This is because so many systems studies have had problems as they inherently attempt to model the real world. This is not acceptable practice in the beliefs implied within soft systems methodology.

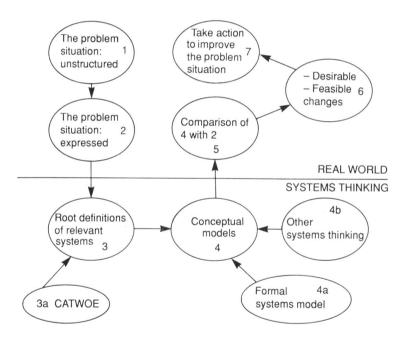

Figure 2.1   Soft systems methodology : the seven-stage model

The methodology is a means of guiding the tackling of real world situations which are perceived as problematical for some of the time by at least one member of that situation. This is the nature of the problem situation. It is discussed more fully in chapter 3. It is necessary to do some analysis of that situation before embarking upon the generation of relevant systems in order that the world of systems thinking can be entered. It is considered of more use if the analysis can be carried out by those within the situation. This means handing over the methodology to those in the perceived problem situation. This is not always easy but is an ideal type prospect for the use of the methodology. The methodology can be used alone but the resultant learning may be very difficult to communicate when this happens.

The seven-stage model encourages the user(s) to undertake an analysis of the problem situation and then to name relevant systems. Systems are relevant in that they help learning about the situation so that debate can occur to help improve the situation. The relevant systems can then be modelled. This is a rigorous use of systems thinking in order to develop models of human activity systems which are purposive models representing ideal type sets of human actions expressed as systems. These are developed through the compilation of 'root definitions', each a concise core description expressing a particular world view of the relevant systems. Root definitions make use of 'CATWOE' elements (customer, actors, transformation, Weltanschauung, owner, environmental constraints) as discussed in chapter 4. Chapter 5 then shows how a root definition can be used to develop a conceptual model, that is, a model of an ideal type human activity system. These are verb-based models which show systemic sets of actions. These models can then be taken back to the real world problem situation and be used in a comparison process between models and perceived reality. This is discussed in chapter 6. Decisions regarding proposed changes then follow; these consider feasible and desirable changes which allow for the recognition of the action needed to improve the problem situation.

There is a persistent problem with the seven-stage model of the methodology. It gives the impression that a series of steps can be carried out in a cookbook fashion and that the problem situation will be changed as a result of this. It is actually just a logical form, but it is often taken as a rational basis for action which will deliver expected results. That is far too much to ask of any methodology. Humans are not so easily compliable as to allow for anyone to adopt a simple set of actions and change what are often deep-seated problem situations. The model is too comforting, it is too rational, and it is often taken for granted. This, along with other reasoning, provided the rationale for changes to this more taken-for-granted form of the model. A new pictorial form of the ideal type model known as soft systems methodology has recently emerged from Checkland and Scholes (1990). This is shown in figure 2.2 below. This book does not work directly to the Checkland and Scholes version but rather introduces it indirectly. Instead, this book still adopts the seven-stage model for pedagogical reasons. To many it is now familiar. A bridge between the two models is required and hopefully this book can help build some of that bridge. However, the same reasoning stands. This book will not provide a cookbook. It can teach and it can illustrate but it cannot provide miracles. That takes individual human effort and ingenuity which cannot be compounded into any methodology!

Figure 2.2   Soft systems methodology 1990

Figure 2.2 shows the same set of actions as figure 2.1, although this may not be immediately obvious. There is still a real world situation of concern which needs analyzing. The discovery period leads on to choices of relevant systems which allow for models to be developed and for comparisons to be made between the models and the real world. The idea is still to debate the action needed to improve the problem situation, and so to go back and re-view the real world situation of concern. The methodology does not appear to be as linear in the second version as it does in the first. There is now a continual flow through, which means that, in principle, the methodology never reaches closure, and this is now far more obvious. The new model is simpler and easier to read but much harder to break down if the newcomer does not understand what is involved in tackling a real world problem situation using soft systems methodology. This book has been written for absolute beginners and so both of the models of the methodology will be referred to. Creating a learning environment demands trying to take very little for granted.

Illustration is one of the best forms of creating a learning environment. Illustration followed by detailed explanation, followed by guidance, followed by discussion, and finally reflection upon illustration. This is the learning path taken by this book. The opening section then must give an illustration. That is the purpose of this present chapter, where an example of the use of the methodology is presented. The many contingent problems that can occur in the use of the methodology are not going to be discussed here but will be discussed in detail in chapter 7. This is a real world example in that it is one study in which one of the authors attempted to use the methodology. The technical aspects of that use are described in this illustrative chapter.

The illustrative study

To call a piece of action intended to change a real world problem situation a 'study' seems strangely inadequate but in this particular case that is exactly what it is. The study was carried out as part of the doctoral work of one of the authors which looked at the cultural aspects of the use of soft systems methodology. The work was carried out by Lynda Davies, who refers personally to it in order to take full responsibility. That is an outmoded statement but in this case it is one which it is necessary to make.

From this point, the rest of the case study becomes personalized. The first person singular, 'I', now intervenes. This may seem strange for some readers, particularly those used to communicating through the media of scientific and technical reports but it is felt necessary for two reasons. First, the use of the methodology was very personal. The fact that the user was a particular kind of person did seem to affect the use in the situation. This is discussed later. Second, this use of the methodology describes events which are interpreted and understood through a qualitative, phenomenological social science stance. Such a stance agrees with personalization of accounts and actively encourages them. I could not be true to my own enquiry beliefs if I denied the use of first person. I hope the reader will accept this and experience some of my understanding of the situation through my accounts in this form. In this way, my experience of acting out the methodology may serve as useful learning for the reader.

The study deals with an evaluation of an information technology (IT) strategy for the British Army. The problem situation was not obvious although my set task was. I was asked to apply my understanding of organizations, and particularly of the human aspects of organizations, to looking at a document which was named as an IT strategy for the Army's use of that technology into the 1990s. I was asked by a senior ranking officer in the Army who was giving me an opportunity to conduct some action research for my PhD work. We both hoped to get something worthwhile out of the study as is the general expectation with action research. I think we both did, but there can be no guarantees of that for either side. That is the first point to realize with the use of soft systems methodology. Because it is not a cookbook with guaranteed results, but merely a set of guidelines to help make sense of action, we could not be sure where we would be going and what we would get out of this excursion. My initiator was a fellow believer in reflective learning in that he believed that any learning was good learning and if we got that out of the study then it must be worthwhile. He was a gem of a person and his guidance made the study worthwhile in some sense. But that is all I can claim.

Analysis of the problem situation

The assumption of the methodology is that there is some form of perceived real world situation which is problematical in some manner for someone. The initial stage in the seven-stage model reflects that assumption. The first analysis deals with the roles of problem solver, problem owner, and decision taker. In this study it was not obvious to whom these roles could be meaningfully attributed. I adopted the role of problem solver. I tried to increase awareness of the methodology in doing this, to 'give it away', and to a very limited extent I was successful. However, this was part of a much larger 'giving away' project that I became involved in, that of teaching the methodology on a major course. That teaching course is referred to throughout this chapter.

When I first started the study, I was not a formal member or associate of the British Army in any way, or at least I did not think that I was, but my husband was an associate in that he was employed as a lecturer at a military college. How firmly that tied me into the organization was not apparent to me at that point. I was still naive about the situation like many beginners in using the methodology, particularly those who are not already directly involved in the situation. I nominated the individual who had offered me the project as the problem owner. This was acceptable as he was in a position where he was responsible for handling the implementation of the strategy in its existing form. He had also been part of the clan (group of a close social network) which had supported the writer of the strategy during the learning involved in the development of the strategy. I, foolishly, did not think too long about the role of decision taker and also attributed this role to him. I had completed the first initial analysis.

I then had to get involved in analyzing the culture of the context of the problem situation. Problem situations do not come in nice neat little boxes. Their boundaries are not always apparent. I did not know what exactly I was meant to be looking at as a 'problem situation'. No problem had been immediately identified and, to some extent, it was my role to uncover potential problems. The problem situation did not leap out and tell me what I should be looking at. I now know that this is commonplace with all attempts at dealing with messy, ill-structured problem situations. At that point I was learning my way through a further use of the methodology, having only used it in earnest once before. All the time, with each use, the users' interpretation changes. This particular illustration cannot give the feel for that change and the contingent uncertainty that comes with it. Anyone who has ever attempted to deal with a problem situation and to use any methodology to help that process will know what I mean. We will bear the same battle scars.

I had to start to structure the social world that I was going to take as relevant in order to begin an analysis of the culture and of the politics. But social worlds are not entities which say "Here is the range, choose your selection". How you yourself are perceived leads to selection of what you will be able to view as part of the problem situation. I had the strategy to work on so I could look at the human resource implications. I also had the context of the military college which, very soon, was employing me on a part-time basis to teach on the one course which it seemed developed the human resources needed to fulfil that strategy. My husband was director of that course.

Talking to members of that course was part of the information collection phase as was the visiting of various departments and seeing different people. The path was chosen by the initiator of the study. I was content with this and I think that is reasonable. No outsider viewing a situation can have better judgement than insiders as to what is a relevant path to learning about a situation. The initiator told me of the problems of developing large-scale information systems and the particular aspects of this problem for the Army. They are vast and I am duty-bound, morally-bound, and legally-bound not to disclose details, having three times signed the Official Secrets Act! One proposal to deal with the idiosyncratic development of new systems was to control the purchasing of new equipment. This meant that anyone who wanted new equipment had to justify it and had to nominate an 'information manager' who could be involved with the implementation of the new technology. As I was told, "Many people want a 'Porsche' when they are asking for new IT. It is my job to look closely at the requirements and to say 'Sorry, but what you need is a Luton van, and that is the best you can hope for, however, you'll have no mechanic, and possibly not even the van!'" The implications of such a strategic move were not immediately obvious to me. They were, however, crucial to the evaluation of the strategy.

The individual who uses soft systems methodology influences what is perceived as the problem situation. That is one very good reason for handing the methodology over to those in the problem situation, so that they can be bound to the problem situation themselves. That handing over process was difficult in this study because the Army does not take on methodologies without formally assessing them and it is not possible to gather together groups for participative handling of the situation, unless that is of the status of a Major General, and in the Guards for that matter! I am female, unfit, an intellectual and about as much of an outsider to the Army officers as it is possible to be. My physical characteristics bear me no political commodities. However, my presence did allow me to come to some level of understanding of the culture. As an outsider, the Army provided many instances of peculiar ritualistic behaviour which seemed strange and incomprehensible to me. They also tend to induce in their staff a willingness to express strong value statements regarding the purpose of the Army. This definitely aided the carrying out of a cultural analysis. I came to realize that the structure of the Army is related to both the bureaucracy and the battlefield. Those who, in principle, are most likely to go to the face of battle and risk death are the heroes. They are the 'teeth' corps. The 'tail' corps are those who wander around safe away from the face of the battle and provide service. IT is part of the service section, it is a 'tail' section and is generally considered of lowly status because of this. Becoming a specialist in IT is not a good career move in the Army. In fact, becoming a specialist in anything but leadership is frowned upon. The primary concern of any training in the Army is that individuals should be able to take up leadership if their formal leader gets killed. Right down the line to the lowliest soldier, that is the case. If an individual is a specialist then he or she is going to be less than capable of taking over this leadership role in battle. Generalism is functional, whilst specialism is anarchic. Career structures make sure that this generalism is protected. Every officer serves a term of around two and a half years in a staff post where he (generally he and rarely she) has to serve at a desk managing the operations and development of the Army as an organization. The next term is spent at a field post where he gets a chance to go through training routines which allow for a simulation of battle. This is the part that most officers love. It is what they joined up for. The staff position is boring but necessary; the field position is exciting and very necessary.

The Army is about battle. The whole culture treats this idea as having material existence – it is *reified*. Mess nights remind people about the heroes who died in the past in battle to defend their corps. The pictures in mess halls turn these battle leaders into heroes of mythical proportions. The accepted everyday truth is that an individual joins the Army for the honour of dying for the Crown, not for the country; a civil war sorted that out. But the funding of the Army occurs through the civil funding process. The Crown does not pay for the Army but the people do and the civil servants are there to make sure that the funding occurs correctly. They are often viewed as the enemy and great games of secrecy are played out to prevent them gaining too much information. The civil service also allocates funding according to the political wishes of the government. This does not always fall in line with the desires of the Army who consider that they understand better than politicians what the needs of the battlefield are. It is not an easy marriage of convenience, and IT had been a major pawn in the discussion of the resource distribution in that marriage. This conflict was reflected in many stories and value expressions. It was also reflected in the clothing of the officers which reflects the loyalty to Crown as paramount.

Representation the problem situation

The cultural analysis was vast and highly complex. However, it did uncover something of the problem situation. The political analysis allowed for the use of commodities to be scrutinized. Resourcing was highly prejudicial according to cultural values – horses or tanks, taking priority over message carriers or IT. The values and the norms were easily related to roles, and the appreciative setting of the Army unfolded. It unfolded from the stance of myself as participant observer. This meant that I tended to hear stories of marital problems and lack of motivation to remain in the Army. I was a female outsider, wife of the director of the major IT training course, and a psychologist, so an easy listener. The role of the problem solver in the use of soft systems methodology can seem more like that of therapist at times as listening is a vital part of that role. Human actions are being dealt with and so human problems and expressions come to the fore. Those expressions come from people's interpretations of the listener. As a wife, I was told problems about family life and was given easy access to the wives who reinforced the stories I was hearing. Relating this to the evaluation of an IT strategy was easier than I at first surmised.

The situation which emerged was one of grave dissatisfaction with a loss of 'perks' in the Army. It was also one of a closed society in which the retention of staff was not considered problematical. Future staff came from the children of present staff, who in turn had been children of past staff. It was nicely closed. But present staff and their families had often interacted more with the wider social community than in the past. This interaction occurred for a number of reasons. The role of women in the late twentieth century has changed, and they do not expect to be tied to the home. Many Army officers' wives have had the benefits of a university education, they both know what it is like to think independently and are well equipped to be able to hold independent careers. The Army takes no account of this. Wives have a place in the Army and families are considered owned by the Army. This is taken for granted. Wives' careers are considered wrong, as they should have a full-time career supporting their husbands. This rather colonialist-style thinking is still dominant in the Army. The perks of being a colonialist-style wife are, however, a thing of the past. Wives do not have servants nor do they have enough finance to be able to send their children through private schooling without considerable financial input from the families themselves. This is not a luxury, for Army families are constantly moved around and children's education gets severely disrupted if they cannot be boarded at private schools. In order to gain the finances to continue with this, wives often have to seek some form of supplementary employment. They could not have a career because they know that they will be moved around regularly; besides, the Army owns them and they have tea party duties to perform. A similar story unfolds regarding playschool facilities and many other 'perks' which appear to be functional rather than luxurious in considering the ongoing continuation of the Army.

Many officers are being faced with a choice. Give up the family life or give up the Army. As many have spent their whole lives in the Army, and their parents before them, they find this choice highly traumatic. The erosion of the perks is not equal throughout the Army either. It is related to the same prejudices as drive the other resource allocation decisions. This means that those who choose to work in IT are likely to experience more stress than those in other corps, as their families are likely to get less of the considerations.

Working on the IT management training course led to another issue being unfolded. The people who graduate from this course are the very information managers that the strategy requires in order to get the new IT implementations working. They are crucial to the success of the strategy. They are leaving, in droves, as soon as they can. Those who come on the course have just come from a staff course where they have spent two and a half years at a desk. The course is held at a military college and attendance is designated as a field position but being a course it is mainly desk work. After the course, individuals go back into a staff course and spend a further two and a half years at a desk. A shortage of actual wars means that active service in the battlefield is rare but sitting at a desk in an office is common. This is not the expected working life that many have joined up for. Also, the desk jobs following the course usually bear no resemblance to any IT related task, as that would encourage specialism and generalism is needed. The new skills are being eroded just when enthusiasm to use them is high. Meanwhile, a government decision has stated that rationalization is required and so outsider consultants are to be used instead of carrying out all tasks internally. A chink in the cultural wall is opening and the disgruntled officers are meeting the outside IT industry where a dire shortage of IT specializing information managers is also being experienced. The outside industries can offer high temptations and many are successful in their attempts to poach military staff into non-military companies. These staff are often at levels in the career structure which means they can not be easily replaced for many years. The strategy really does seem in real danger.

The problem situation has now been 'discovered' or at least analyses allow it to emerge. The expression of this problem situation, the rich picture, is shown in figure 2.3 below. This serves as a means of condensing all the information that has been gathered into a simple expression of the problem situation. It makes for easy checking when considerations of relevant systems and comparisons are carried out. The next stage is to generate relevant systems so that attempts at changing the problem situation can be made. In looking at this situation there are many potential relevant systems. In this illustration only one will be developed in detail. Relevant systems named included a divorce enhancing system, an IT strategy immobilizing system, a family managing system, a culture maintaining system, a culture destroying system, and a key personnel shortage maintaining system. The last of these is developed in detail.

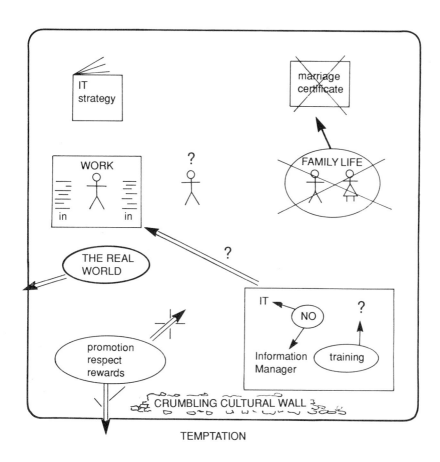

Figure 2.3   Rich Picture of the Problem Situation

The development of the systems thinking

Moving into the systems thinking activity occurs as relevant systems are named. It is important now to stop referring back to the real world of the perceived problem situation. This is because that referential process starts again in the comparison phase after the ideal type systems models have been developed. The ideal type models developed should be logically closed and complete. They do not contain anything but the logical set of activities which are the named system. This means that the expansion of that naming into the root definition (the concise core description expressing a particular world view of the relevant systems) must be carefully controlled and consideration of real world consequences must be put out of mind. This is not easy. It is probably the most difficult but the most important part of the technical aspect of developing and using models of human activity systems. Some writers on soft systems methodology refer to human activity systems as real world entities when they are discussing the problem situation. This is wrong and it is lazy and erroneous thinking. Soft systems methodology demands controlled thinking in the systems thinking phases. It is here that models which are representations of human activity systems are developed. They are not models of human action nor of any aspect of the real world. They are models relevant to learning about the real world. Having named the relevant systems, the question of relevancy is no longer addressed in the world of systems thinking. Now the modeller has to act as a logical machine and develop the models free from consideration of the problem context.

The named relevant system which is being developed here is that of a key personnel shortage maintaining system. Having named it in brief form, it is now necessary to develop the name more fully into a root definition. Chapter 4 goes into detail to explain how this happens. The first step is to develop a CATWOE analysis (customer, actors, transformation, Weltanschauung, owner, environmental constraints). A full explanation of the terms used in the CATWOE analysis is given in chapter 4, along with a discussion of its purposes. From the CATWOE analysis, a root definition can be developed. An alternative approach is to develop the root definition and then to use the CATWOE analysis to check that the root definition is accurately constructed. This can be used to develop the root definition or to check the root definition. In the present illustration the CATWOE analysis is used as the basis for the development of the root definitions and then used to check whether the definitions are complete.

CATWOE analysis:

C = customer = military officers

A = actors = military personnel

T = transformation = unmaintained key personnel shortage

$\implies$ maintained key personnel shortage

W = Weltanschauung = maintaining a key personnel shortage
    is a worthwhile thing to do

O = owner = the military

E = environmental constraints = regulations, beliefs, resources

The root definition is:

A military-owned, military officer-used system to maintain a shortage of key personnel by identifying a shortage, training personnel to continue in that capacity, using the trained personnel in jobs other than those trained for, allowing the personnel to question their personal futures, allowing them to interact with other forms of society, losing the personnel, and recognizing the continual shortage of personnel. All this is carried out in a context in which organizational rules are unchallenged as irrefutable beliefs and the environment is being constrained by the rules, beliefs, resource limitations, and development policies.

Checking the root definition back against the CATWOE analysis shows that the definition is coherent and full. This means that it is ready to be used as the basis of the development of a conceptual model. The verbs are underlined so that modelling may begin. The conceptual model is shown in figure 2.4 below.

The main activities which are immediately identifiable out of the root definition are those of:

1. Identify shortage of key personnel
2. Train personnel
3. Use those personnel in jobs other than those trained for
4. Allow personnel to question their personal futures
5. Allow them to interact with other forms of society
6. Lose personnel
7. Recognize continual shortage of personnel

These activities have to be expanded upon in order to allow for the completeness of the development of the conceptual model.

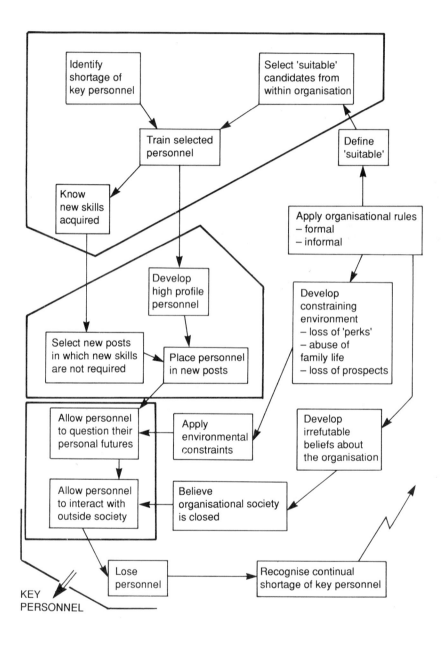

Figure 2.4   Conceptual Model of a System for maintaining Key Personnel

Other activities are necessary because they are implied by the environmental constraints. This means that "Develop constraining environment", "Develop irrefutable beliefs", "Believe organizational society is closed", and "Apply organizational rules" come from consideration of the environmental constraints mentioned in the CATWOE analysis and the root definition. Other activities come from breaking down the main activities in the root definition and then looking at whether logically the activities can move from one to the other. This is how missing activities implied in the root definition are noted such as "Define 'suitable'". Without that activity the selection of candidates would not be tied into the application of organizational rules. Again "Apply environmental constraints" is necessary in order to link together the development of the constraining environment and the allowing of personnel to challenge their personal futures. This forming of the conceptual model relates only to the root definition and the logic of the formal systems model to gain completeness. No activities are imported from thinking about the real world of the problem situation. This conceptual model does not show the monitoring and controlling activities which go on but these would link into the boundary of the system and show how the system is maintaining itself over time. They are part of the model but just not shown in this particular diagrammatic representation of the model for purposes of frugality and concerns regarding clarity of presentation.

Having developed one conceptual model a fully developed study would now develop others from the named relevant systems. As this study is just being used for the purposes of illustration, space limits further presentation of conceptual models and root definitions. It should be noted though that it is unwise to just rely on information from a comparison with one model.

Comparison and action

Comparison can take place in a number of ways as discussed in chapter 6. The model as a whole can be generally discussed, or the model can be treated in parts as sets of activities and those activities individually compared in a comparison chart. The latter exercise would be unnecessarily cumbersome and so a general comparison will be made. In looking at the real world of the problem situation, the model seems to fit too close for comfort. It seems that if the Army had designed its organization to lose key personnel on a continual basis, it had achieved an outstandingly good design! It seems that this system is not really desirable to this problem situation, as the logic of the actions appears to work extremely well, but the Weltanschauung expressed is not one with which the Army has much sympathy. After all, the expression of the problem situation is that the strategy will fail if this key personnel shortage is not reversed.

Cultural feasibility considerations are more shocking. It seems that the culture of the Army would uphold many of the activities. In fact, cultural beliefs are strongly reinforcing the activities. One crucial activity to maintain the flow of the system is that of "Select new posts in which new skills are not required". This activity is central to the culture of the Army as it relates to leadership capability in the battlefield. To advise the members of that situation simply to stop doing this would definitely be culturally infeasible. Another activity which is central to the operations of the system is that of "Develop irrefutable beliefs about the organization". This is another activity which it is difficult to challenge. It would have to be a very powerful change instigator who could attempt to deal with changing that activity. However, the process of exposure, which is central to soft systems methodology, could start to tackle some of the beliefs. The real challenge is to the degree to which the beliefs are truly irrefutable. If they are absolutely so then any exposure will go unheeded. It will not expose. It is probably easier to expose the activity which shows close similarity when compared with observation and that is "Believe organizational society is closed". This belief can be exposed even if changes to that belief cannot be dealt with directly. The development of the constraining environment also shows a close similarity in comparison between the human activity system model and the perceived real world problem situation. This appears to be a potential area for intervention. Furthermore, the realization occurs that the activity dealing with the application of the organizational rules can be used for positive effects, that is, to destroy this apparition which is close to that of the undesirable system. This shows that comparison can be used to expose the system and what holds it together and so use this knowledge to break down any real world similarities which are found but considered undesirable.

The use of this comparison leads to a need to bring the learning from the debate between the situation and the models into the forum of the situation. So far, only the comparison has been given, as there is no development of partici-pative structures to allow for a more open debate. This closed nature of the debate is necessitated in part by the operational preferences of the Army and in part by the manner in which the study has jointly been directed by myself and the initiator. The initiator, in his role as problem owner, requested a formal documentation to discuss the learning which had occurred so far from the study. This documentation is given in the form of a short report in which the situation as seen is briefly discussed. No use of rich pictures, root definitions, or conceptual models is included in the report as it is considered that this will hinder a more general reading of the document. This is generally not a problem. The modelling techniques are only adopted to help structure the debate. They do not have to be made visible.

The comparison has highlighted that the constraining environment is a problem which it may be possible to deal with. The wives provide a possible forum for this. A suggestion made in the report is that a formal task group be set up to look at the situation of Army families, and to examine the effects of that situation on staff morale and subsequent loss of personnel. Another suggestion comes from comparing the activities of selecting, training, and developing suitable personnel to turn them into high profile personnel. This issue of retaining the high profile status of the trained personnel after re-entry into the working environment of the organization is seen to be an important issue. It seems that the application of organizational rules can help with this situation. The rules state that high profile, and valued, development of staff can be noted by regalia worn on uniforms. This is vital to the values of the Army personnel as all forms of regalia are part of history and so important to their everyday lives. That is crucial to the culture of the Army. It is suggested that a new regalia form connected to passing the training course can be added to the uniform. This means that the skills gained on the course will be valued as they will be signified as important in the history of the Army. This is a weighty request.

The process which followed is one which caused severe problems for this author. I was prevented from any further contact with the study after a single phone call. This is discussed further in chapter 7. By being a member of the military college, I was able to see the process unfold after this rather stunning exclusion. Some time later the strategy report was revised and included the two additions which this study had resulted in suggesting. The exposure process had resulted in a useful output for those in the problem situation. The trap had been perceived regarding the issues in that situation. The trap for the user of the methodology had not. This is important for any user. The methodology, being a set of principles for action, will not guide the user on how to be aware and deal with particular situations. That requires wisdom which is gained, in part, from this study, but is not there during the study. The learning process of soft systems methodology occurs in many forms and it is erroneous to forget that users of the methodology are always part of the problem situation, they will have to assume certain responsibilities for their actions and deal with their consequences, and thereby they also will learn from the experience.

This illustrative study has merely provided a first view of the methodology. Each of the next four chapters develops in greater detail the different parts of the methodology. The seventh chapter then returns to this study to reflect upon the use of the methodology as well as looking at change and action in problem situations.

Discussion issues

1. The problem that the Army has is one of managing a limited supply of human resources. Do you think that the Army's problem can be found in other organizations? Discuss how the Army situation is:

   (i)   similar to other organizational situations

   (ii)   different from other organizational situation

   Use the notions of culture, politics, and roles to do this.

2. Discuss to what extent the problems are related to technology or related to information management.

3. Discuss whether you think using differently named relevant systems might have helped the user of the methodology to handle the situation better.

Exercises

1. Looking at the description of the problem situation, imagine that you have to present this to your immediate superior. Would you change the style of presentation? Change and enhance the rich picture to include more of the key relevant factors which you can find. Leave out those which you think could be problematical. Could you structure it differently to improve its informative nature?

2. From the first exercise generate at least two further named relevant systems. Why do you consider that they are relevant? Discuss these with those around you who are also using this book.

3. Looking at the conceptual model and reading the material which discusses the problem situation, consider if there are any further suggestions for change which could be made. Relate these directly to the comparison of the model with the interpretation of the problem situation given in this chapter. What problems do you think you would have if you were trying to structure the debate so that change could occur in this situation? Discuss, with the benefits of hindsight, how you may have gone about things differently.

4. As you progress through the book, use this case study to try out the different techniques that you come across. The book is only partially linear in its development. It is worth returning to this chapter as you learn more, to see if you view it differently as you do return.

Suggested reading

Checkland, P.B., *Systems Thinking, Systems Practice*, Wiley, Chichester, 1981.
    This is the original key book on soft systems methodology. It is an important source book in the development of the methodology.

Checkland, P.B. and Scholes, J., *Soft Systems Methodology in Action*, Wiley, Chichester, UK, 1990.
    This is the updated version of the above book which is particularly useful as it discusses the use of the methodology.

3 Problem situations

- *Problems, situations, and traps*
- *Perceiving the trap*
- *Analysis of the situation*
- *The problem content and the problem solving system*
- *Checklist for starting analysis*
- *The culture of the problem situation*
- *Analysis of the culture*
- *Political analysis*
- *Appreciation, world views, and choosing relevant systems*

We are now moving on to look at soft systems methodology in detail. This particular chapter deals with the first part of any learning process, the initial finding out phase. In order to learn, we must enquire and this means analyzing the situation as it stands. This is probably the most demanding part of any learning process. It is here that what is informative, and what is not, is continually being negotiated between individuals in that situation. It is where relevant information is constructed so that the situation can be appreciated. This chapter deals with ways in which this can be achieved within the framework of the methodology.

Problems, situations, and traps

Situations and problems are not nicely solid objects that can be grasped hold of, inspected, and reconstructed, but are creations which are formed by individuals and groups of individuals. This means that they cannot easily and objectively be found and analyzed down into constituent parts. They are created as meaningful constructs contingent upon particular times, places, and sets of purposes for their interpretation. If the user of any approach to problem or issue management enters a situation of concern with a view to finding the problem, analyzing it and, from that analysis, finding and applying a solution, then they are likely to be disappointed, frustrated or even just confined to acting in ignorance. The rhetoric that takes it seem sensible that problems are to be found and solved is inappropriate for organizational life. Problems are very often ill-formed, messy, wicked, transient, varying in salience and relevance, and always contingent. Problems belong to situations; the two are inseparable. Any attempt to manage problems must manage situations. It is because of this realization, gained from practical experience, that Checkland and his colleagues at Lancaster took the conscious decision to refer not to problems, but only to problem situations, when referring to the contexts most appropriate to the relevant use of soft systems methodology.

Problem situations are part of the real world of social action. This concept, called a 'real world' as a social construct, is a conundrum. It does not have any objective existence that we can be certain about. Rather, it is constructed by people taking action together. In doing so they construct a continually changing idea of the real world and act upon that idea, thus constantly changing it in their attempts at understanding it. We all do this. I am doing it now and you are doing it in reading this text. The complex ability of human beings to construct, challenge, play with, and externalize ideas is seen in its extreme when the construction of everyday social reality is looked at. The town planner constructs a view of a reality which she/he hopes will be useful and desirable for the people of that town. Any planner working alone is likely to get lost in his own ideas and that is why it is a good strategy to construct the ideas of a town plan whilst interacting with others. In that way, the resultant reality is not so shocking, nor so far removed from the socially developed desires of the community. However, the fantasies which some town planners build are not always constructed through a great variety of social interaction, and the end result can be less than satisfactory for those who live in it. This creates problem situations. The lack of sharing of ideas, the lack of sharing of the construction process of those ideas, and the lack of clarity of expression, leading to a lack of common understanding, and a lack of sharing of key values, hopes and aspirations, can all lead to problem situations which seem insurmountable. People have to communicate to overcome the issues inherent in these situations and that is not always as easy or as trivial as it may at first seem.

Why is this construction of the idea of a real world so problematical if we do it all the time? Most of the time we do it unreflectively, and we just muddle through. Sometimes muddling through is not good enough, and those involved in the situation experience its problematical nature so acutely that they find it

hard just to carry on with the muddle. The images of the real world being acted
upon are insufficient. They need clarification and rethinking. They need action
aimed strategically at improving them. It is at this point that it is necessary to
stop and think about the consequences of the view of the real world which has
just been put forward.

Creating ideas about reality is both a mundane and an awesome concept. It
is mundane because we do it all the time. It is awesome because once we think
about this concept then we realize that everything is constructed through ideas of
reality. Even the idea of the construct of an idea of reality! We cannot get away
from it. If it starts to go wrong, to cause problems, we are trapped inside it. We
are trapped by our own processes of trying to make sense of it, that is, we are
trapped by being human. It is vicious but unavoidable. This idea of the trap of
making sense was developed by Sir Geoffrey Vickers and is fundamental to the
notion of the problem situation in soft systems methodology. A trap is a trap as
long as we cannot see a way out of it. This is a profound idea, although it can
seem obvious, too obvious, and therefore trivial. Vickers talks of a lobster which
is trapped in a pot, not because of the physical structures of the lobster but
because the lobster perceives that it is trapped. Physically the lobster is capable
of escape but intellectually it is incapable of seeing that and so it does not try.
Because the lobster is supposedly without a self concept, it cannot reflect upon
its situation and try to rethink of itself in an alternative situation and from that
learn how to take action to get out of the trap. Lobsters are trapped into being
lobsters and so cannot self-reflect. Human traps are different. They allow for self-
reflection as a way of managing the trap. This can allow for the trap to be
reviewed and perceived as something which can be overcome. Action to put that
idea into practice can then follow. Humans can view problems as opportunities,
so long as they can construct the ideas of reality to make that feasible. It is easy
really. We just need to understand how to achieve this management of the idea
of traps and so take action to get out of those traps and, hopefully, how to avoid
getting into too many other problematical traps. That intention is at the basis of
soft systems methodology when used in action.

Perceiving the trap

If you cannot see that you are in a trap, then there is no way left of getting out
of it, apart from that of blind chance. However, seeing the trap allows you to ask
if there is any way to get out of it and so we can manage the process of exit

from the trap rather than just waiting to see what fate dishes out. If we take it that the trap is a construction, an idea, then reflecting upon that construction can help to change it from a trap to a way out. Further, if we take it that the trap is socially constructed, then we have to look at the socially held idea of the trap and how a group of people can get out of it. We cannot solve the enigma of the trap alone because we did not create it alone. We must learn about the trap together and so learn how to manage the exit. This means that the perception of the trap must be done as a social act not as an individual one. Communication is a process in which new ideas are constructed, so communication must be acted out as part of the process, not as an afterthought once the 'solution' has been dreamed up. By that time the construction of the idea of the trap has probably changed and so the individually derived solution would be redundant anyway.

Communicating as part of a social group, when the world seems so problematical, is not an easy process. Guidelines to help with the perception of the trap are useful. In soft systems methodology these come as part of the "analysis of the problem situation" phase. Do not be fooled. This is not analysis in the sense of deriving a pure form of the problem as a first step towards solution. The analytical process is not abstract but contingent. It comes from being involved in that situation and, hence, being part of the problem situation. Users of soft systems methodology are actors not passive observers. However, the methodology does provide analytical help in the form of guidelines as to what are useful considerations for starting the perceptual processes needed to enable change. These guidelines come in three forms, and are presented and discussed next.

Analysis of the situation

Any situation may be understood through looking at it as people playing roles. This comes from the sociological theory that we are all actors playing out dramas, and is the basis of role theory as discussed by Goffmann. It provides useful metaphors for understanding social life, that is, people making sense of reality by acting together in order to construct ideas of reality. Soft systems methodology formally presents various roles which it is useful to consider in order to start the process of making sense of the trap of the problem situation. These roles come into two forms, those which are directly involved in the problem situation and understand it in that form, and those which are deliberately seeking to change the problem situation. These are the roles of the problem owner and the problem solver, and they are viewed as belonging to two interacting conceptual frameworks, the problem content and the problem solving system. The conceptual frameworks are helpful in making sense of the process of trying to understand the problem situation in order to change it.

The problem content and the problem solving system

Any user of soft systems methodology holds some form of belief that there is a problem situation. This situation has certain aspects to it which are discovered through looking at those who can be viewed playing certain roles. Whoever views this situation wishes to change it and so seeks to play a problem solving role. The means which connect the viewing of the problem situation to the desire to solve the problems of the situation is that of soft systems methodology. This view of the two different sets of roles and their relation to the methodology are shown in figure 3.1 below.

The key role adopted by those using the concept of the problem solving system is that of the problem solver. This role can be held by one or many. It is the role which is logically implied by actions which aim to tackle the problem situation. There is some form of inherent belief held by this role which is that the problem situation is of such a nature that it may be tackled, and that the aim of tackling it is to try to make it less problematical. The role only aims to solve the problem insofar as it directs whoever takes on that role to the view that problem situations may be improved. The role is not an individual, rather, it is a set of guidelines for action which any individual can adopt. Those guidelines state that the belief must be held that the situation is problematical and that it can be improved. It is the role of the perceptive optimist! It simply states that anyone adopting it has made a realization that there is a problem situation and has taken the first level of commitment to try to tackle that problem situation with a desire to take action to improve it. Those wishing to provoke the problem situation, no matter how heroic their intent may seem, cannot be said to be adopting the role of the problem solver. The problem solver wishes to make sense of the problem situation and to use the concept of system in that sense-making process, and so adopts the methodology in order to do this. The role of problem solver is often talked about as if one person goes into a problem situation and acts as a lone champion by seeking to change that situation. This is a heroic but also a rather foolish interpretation. The heroic actions of seeking changes are better if adopted by many, and especially by those within the problem situation. This is because of the construction of the idea of reality discussed earlier in this chapter. It is now recognized, and actively stressed, that the role of the problem solver includes that of the negotiator of social reality, and that the negotiation process must occur as a social process. This means that the role of the problem solver is concerned with structuring the communication of the debate for change, so that those within the problem situation adopt the role of problem solver themselves. This is challenging but necessary. It takes the emphasis away from the expert problem solver who oversees the situation and provides opinion. Instead, it stresses the role of problem solver as communication manager, aiding the participative process of sense-making that helps the perception of the trap and the consequential actions necessary for dealing with that trap. Problem solvers are involved, they do not just sit on the sidelines making judgements.

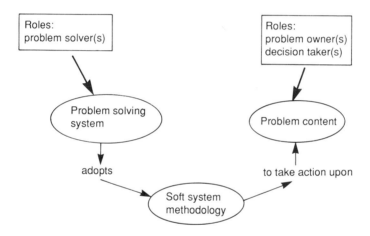

Figure 3.1 Problem content and problem solving system

Adopting the role of problem solver means that the methodology is taken up. The user of the methodology is guided by the principles for action it provides. These are expanded upon throughout this book and include the analyses discussed later in this chapter as well as the use of conceptual models of relevant systems to aid the problem solving process. That process deals with making sense of the situation so that, through debate, the trap of the problem situation can be understood and tackled. The different views of that situation can then be clarified with the aid of systems concepts. These concepts are found in the conceptual models but also in the systemic nature of the methodology itself. The methodology is a form of appreciative system. It helps decision-making, which is the basis of informed action. The appreciative system is a framework for understanding the process of sense-making within which we are all constrained to act due to our human actions of seeing the world through socially negotiated realities, with both the reality constructs and the processes of negotiation forming subtle and complex traps. Appreciating helps us to see those traps and so to be more perceptive in our attempts to overcome them.

The problem solving system is a form of appreciative system, but only insofar as it holds an inherent desire to change the situation through understanding it. Appreciation must lead to action for change. The problem solving system is a metaphor for action dealing with the use of the methodology. This is different from the methodology itself which is just a set of guidelines or principles for action. An example may help to clarify the distinction between on the one hand principles as something that has the potential to guide action, and on the other the use of those principles in action.

As an example, let us look at typing. I am typing. I understand the tapping of fingers on a keyboard as typing and am doing this for the purpose of writing. This is the use of two sets of principles, those of writing and those of typing. I have idiosyncratic ways of applying those principles (I am a four-finger typist and I write in my own particular style). Those idiosyncrasies can be described as using the principles of typing and writing in order to communicate. The process is not the principles but merely the use of those principles. I used to study the cognitive aspects of writing. I looked at the principles of writing as cognitive constructs or linguistic forms. I dealt with principles not idiosyncrasies. Engineers designing keyboards look at the ergonomic principles of the manual aspects of typing in relation to problems of dexterity. Linguists look at the stylistic aspects of the principles of text production. All can be applied to my actions of writing to seek to understand them. Equally, I can apply those principles to try and write or type better but my actions of writing and typing do not equate with the principles. They can simply be described as using them. In this same manner, soft systems methodology is a set of principles for action, not the idiosyncrasies of action itself.

Likewise, the problem solving system is merely a way of describing an appreciation of the problem situation through adoption of the role of problem solver. It is a metaphor for using the methodology, and when seen in action can be highly idiosyncratic. The principles state that I, as problem solver, must adopt a view of the problem situation as one which can and must be changed by action which is developed through using the methodology. In the world of actions I can do this by many different manners and means. Real world action allows for variety, whilst principles are a limited set to apply to that variety. The real world of action is not a limited set. This is why it is so difficult to compare one attempt to use the methodology in the problem solving role with any other attempt. The idiosyncrasies are obvious whilst the principles are more opaque. See the work of Checkland and Scholes (1990) to expand upon this argument.

The problem solver adopts the methodology to take action upon, or to improve, or to seek to change the problem situation. This is where the notion of the problem content and the roles relevant to that aspect come into play. The problem content is the bounded view of the problematical nature of the situation. It is bounded through debate and through some form of consensus. The problem content has been developed over time and so has some form of relevant history. This is discussed more fully in the next section. There are also key roles in the problem content which demand consideration. These are the roles of the problem owner(s) and the decision taker(s).

The role of the decision taker is the least problematical of the two and so is considered first. In any problem situation action must be capable of being taken to improve that problem situation. This means that someone must have the power and/or authority to decide on appropriate forms of action. This is fundamental to the role of the decision taker. It would be wrong to imply a sense of organizational hierarchy to this role. The decision taker could be a group of people who are directly involved in the situation just as easily as someone who has authoritative power to change things because of his position in the formal hierarchy. Using the methodology involves a process of challenging who could adopt this role. Action will be required, so this consideration is vital. Consideration of the role can also uncover that there are many different forms of power structures within the situation and, hence, many different potential decision takers. Processes to deal with this need debating. The purpose is not to create a unitary view of the situation in which a single, solitary decision taker is identified, but to look carefully at the debate which has unfolded a problem situation and to ask what are the perspectives of that debate and who could adopt the role of decision taker to help the dialectical processes of that debate in leading to improvement and change. The decision taker is then a heroic role in the sense of being crucial to the process of the debate in bravely seeking to uncover, challenge, and hence provide the potential and means for change. The decision taker must be capable of being critical about the situation and looking for alternative constructions. This is the form of action which leads to change. It is probably far more effective to encourage a multiple-person view of the decision taker rather than trying to hand the role over to individuals. It is vital to realize that the decision taker is a role attributed to people and not *de facto* any one individual.

The role of the problem owner has proved to be more confusing. Many times we have witnessed despairing students saying that they are held up in their analyses because they cannot attribute the role of problem owner firmly to any one individual, and end up adopting the role themselves. It has to be kept in mind that this is a role. There is no one absolute problem owner in any problem situation. It is simply a necessity to act as if that role is present. Someone perceives that there is some form of problematical nature in the situation. They take ownership of the concept of problem situation. This taking up of ownership is part of the perceptual aspect of the use of the methodology. Perceiving that there is a trap is part of the self-reflective process of appreciating the situation which is necessary in order to be able to challenge that situation critically, and so aim to create change to improve it. The role of problem owner simply denotes whose perception of the problematical nature of the situation is being discussed at some moment in the dialectical process of learning called soft systems methodology. The role is often over-intellectualized. It is fluent and negotiable and only there to help clarify whose point of view is being explored. That in itself is powerful, but not as harrowing as some users of the methodology have taken it to be. Generally, it is wise to use the methodology as a formal process to help in the learning process of appreciation through dialectical debate. To pin it down to absolute forms of role-dependent behaviour, attributable to particular types of individuals, is erroneous and counter-productive. It over-complicates a quite simple view of change, that is that change occurs through learning from debate. Searching for the one true problem owner dismisses the fluidity of that learning process and resorts to the view of problems as something which are absolute, can be found, and can be attributed to specific individuals. Attribute the role for clarification purposes, not for classification and absolutist reasons. The role is necessary only in order to establish a point of view at a particular time in the learning process. It follows, therefore, that in a dialectical process it is likely that there will be many problem owners, one of whom may well need to be the formal user of the methodology, at least for some of the time. In this way, the roles of problem solver and problem owner may be held by the same individuals, as may the role of decision taker. That is the nature of roles which are socially attributable labels of convenience that clarify the consequences of viewpoints. That is all they need to be.

Checklist for starting analysis

Any use of soft systems methodology starts by looking at the relationship between the problem context and the problem solving system. This process can be described in the form of a checklist which can then be used as a guide for starting the use of the methodology. This checklist given here is to be used as a guide. It does not have to be followed; rather it is there to help when needed.

Someone has started this analysis by asking for some form of help, so ask:
1. Who is the initiator?
2. Is the initiator acting alone or for a group of people?
   Others have concerns. These are problem owners, so ask:
3. Who are the problem owners?
4. What are the expressed concerns of the problem owners?
   Someone must have the power to eventually alter the situation. These are the decision takers, so ask:
5. Who are the decision takers?
6. Why do the occupiers of these roles regard the situation as in need of change?
7. What do these roles expect of the individual entering the situation to help?
   This individual is likely to be the user of soft systems methodology. It is a role and so can be held by many people, including the initiator, problem owners, and decision takers.

This checklist helps users to get going at the start of a soft systems analysis by providing some very general guidelines regarding important roles in the learning process.

The culture of the problem situation

Culture is probably the greatest example of a human trap found in everyday life. Cultures are imperceptible influencers of everyday behaviour and values. They create a consensus of thought without the reflective debate of useful consensus. They construct the framework whereby everyday social life is constructed. They are the mysteriously hidden blueprints of traps, and can render opaque the nature of those traps. If the perception of traps is crucial to learning ways out of those traps, then perception of cultures is of paramount importance. This is crucial not only to the real world aspects of the methodology principles but also to the use of the methodology in problem situations.

Every problem situation has a history. Part of that history has led to the development of beliefs about what are meaningful roles, values, and norms. Vickers argues that these interact to form the basis of the appreciative setting (see figure 3.2). This appreciative setting may also be termed the culture of the situation.

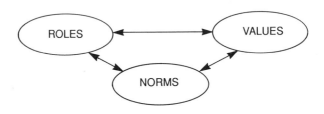

Figure 3.2   Vickers' notion of the appreciative setting

In any situation it is necessary for individuals to adopt and enact roles. This means that all the behaviour we both see and experience everyday is role related. Roles are frameworks for action which we use all the time and, in doing so, change them to some extent. This is because roles are expectations regarding behaviour. They are rule based but also ambiguous and so can be reinterpreted in part. We learn how to be part of social life through role-dependent behaviour. This means that teachers play roles with their students as do managers with workers, systems analysts with users and computer technicians, and parents with children. Roles make social life less surprising so that we can go about carrying out the actions of our everyday world without constantly wondering about the implied intentions of other people's behaviour. However, roles can be challenged. Roles provide the rule base from which social life is played out. Those rules have been socially constructed. Sometimes the roles are ill understood, as in the case where new forms of social interaction are needed. For example, the 'patient therapist' is not formally just a nurse, but has other tasks to perform whilst she/he can justifiably refuse certain tasks associated with general nursing. However, the role has been newly named to deal with specialized forms of nursing, like that of nursing short stay mentally ill patients. The new naming leads to ambiguity in role-expected behaviour, and the boundaries of that task-related behaviour have to be negotiated. This leads to the opening up of the complexity of the social life so that the new rules for behaviour can be discussed and tried. The simplicity which previous forms of role give cannot be so easily applied to new role forms, as they are still being negotiated.

Sometimes role-related behaviour is required to change because of general social changes. The changing role of the father in the latter half of the twentieth century illustrates this. This role is symbolized in many forms, such as through media reinterpretation of the father as gentle baby-handler. This has been reflected in a more tangible form in the baby-changing rooms which are now seen to be called "mothers' room/fathers' room". It is unwise to take role-dependent behaviour too much for granted, as social behaviour, being fluid, is constantly being challenged and changed. But for the purposes of complexity management of the day-to-day enactment of roles is generally taken-for-granted and shows few surprises.

Roles are not God-given. They are socially formed. The formation of roles comes from perceptions of what behaviour ought to be associated with various classifications or types. This, again, is for the simplification of social life on an everyday basis. However, what is not always obvious is that the classification process is value laden, that is, it bears hidden assumptions as to what is right or wrong. This is how roles and values are interlinked. In this manner it is values which help to form roles by indicating what is correct behaviour. However, the formation process goes both ways. When roles are enacted they create reactions from both those adopting the roles and those who are in the presence of the role actors. They create value-laden responses to the hidden values expressed in the roles. Not everyone agrees with the changing role of the father, and the reaction can be one of negation of the new forms of behaviour. Values are difficult to change, whereas roles can be renegotiated quickly. Some organizational problems have found that work roles can be reviewed and described as different actions, but the value stances of those in the roles stops the newly negotiated role actions from being accepted within the work situation. Roles and values need to be teased out as conceptually separate processes for an analysis of the culture of any problem situation to be understood.

Another factor of the triad of the appreciative setting is that of norms of behaviour. Roles are socially constructed contracts for expectations of behaviour. Values are the individually developed expectations regarding the salience of different forms of expression of social behaviour. Norms are the formats for behaviour; they may or may not be role related, but often are. It is the non-norm-related forms of behaviour which can be most problematical because they are often difficult to perceive. It is norms of behaviour which have individuals expressing that "we don't do it that way here", which can cause disarray for the newcomer to a situation. Norms are socially negotiated expectations of behaviour which become the moral codes for actions. It is the norms of behaviour which newcomers often break, even when the common values have been made clear and the roles have been explained. It is norms which separate insiders from outsiders, create informal hierarchies, come to be negotiated during power clashes, and lead to culture shock for newcomers. It is norms which can resist change because they are so often implicit. Norms substantiate values and are heavily value laden. They can describe and support formal roles, but they can also be used to undermine formal work roles. They are a vital part of any culture and so must be a vital part of the cultural analysis of any appreciative setting. Norms create the mind-set which dictates the correct form of appreciation; in this manner they are extremely powerful and need uncovering so that conflicts can be surfaced and the open communicative context of dialectical debate is made possible. It is only when this is made possible can the learning process which soft systems methodology creates be facilitated. No methodology can go against the roles, values, and norms of the culture of the appreciative setting of the problem situation.

Analysis of the culture

The effective use of soft systems methodology depends upon the user(s) having an appreciative understanding of the problem situation. Problem situations often occur because of conflicts inherent in different interpretations of actions, intentions, and consequences. The principles of the methodology infer this by their reference to Vickers' concept of the appreciative system. However, the principles give no direct guidelines regarding the analysis of any culture. This is not surprising. There are many aspects to the use of the methodology which are not covered in detail by the methodological principles, for example, different forms of comparison or the taking of action to improve the situation. These emphases are noted to be related to 'real world' rather than to 'systems thinking' principles. Whereas it is a relatively straightforward matter to make clear the principles in the formal development of systems thinking, it is far more difficult, and far less applicable, to present clear principles regarding the management of real world activities. The real world is less formal and more complex than the world of systems thinking. Principles have to be open and flexible to allow for the contingent variety in the real world. Principles in directing actions which deal with specifically real world aspects of any methodology, by necessity, must be brief and general. Soft systems methodology is no different in this respect and so the real world aspects of the methodology are only very general guidelines, whereas the systems thinking aspects are far more complete and absolute. This is not to say that there are no standards by which to measure good or bad real world aspects of the use of the methodology. The principles of real world actions say that the models of human activity systems must be used as ideal-type metaphors, not as descriptions of real world entities. Action to change must seek to create learning enhanced by the dialectic of debate, and the view of reality must be that of a socially-constructed world of discourse and action which is value laden, ambiguous, multiple in perspectives, and constantly changing. Also, the inherent belief of the methodology is that models are the means by which systems concepts can be used to enhance the learning process of change, and that those models are developed as relevant to that learning process.

Understanding of the culture of the situation is something that is to be gained through the development of the understanding of the appreciative setting of the problem situation. However, there are some guidelines for cultural analysis which may be usefully imported from anthropology. There are difficulties with cultural analysis, though. It is very difficult for those in the situation to examine their own culture without help. This is because the culture has become commonplace to its members. They take it for granted, yet it affects their everyday lives by structuring the relevance of objects in their world. The world of culture is a world of symbols and artifacts but these are just the aspects of the world which cultural members use daily in their interactions, without self-reflective questioning. They create the cognitive framework for thinking, decision-making, and interaction. They are the interpretative framework which makes up the lexicon by which their everyday actions are understood. What is more, these frameworks are developed through historical episodes which are usually forgotten or enacted as theatrical forms rather than as reflections of their original form. Cultural history becomes a reconstructed cultural form in and of itself. Culture is the semantic frame which moulds the meaning contexts of the everyday lives of cultural members. Culture is present because it is continually reconstructed, thus making it more powerful than ever as it is replayed as meaningful on a daily basis. If the culture is not understood then it can create the fundamental framework by which the trap can be continually enacted. Making visible the culture can make visible the trap and so enhance the possibility of overcoming that trap.

If members cannot 'see' culture very easily, then how is it to be exposed to them? The obvious solution is to have an outsider point it out to them. This can be problematical on two accounts. First, the outsider is unlikely to be able to interpret the culture until the meaningful framework is found to which members are privy. This means the outsider understanding as an insider, which creates the possibility of the outsider becoming an insider and so also taking the culture for granted. Second, the outsider is unlikely to be able to interpret the culture as the insider members do, and so is likely to get it wrong, or have their interpretations rejected. This makes cultural analysis a difficult task if it is conducted by outsiders for insiders. Another alternative is for those who are already cultural members, and those who are entering the culture actively, to seek to interpret the culture and learn it together. This is using a combined form of exposure, exposing the new to the culture, and exposing the culture through challenging it by asking what the symbolic forms mean. This is the manner which seems most appropriate to soft systems methodology. It is by taking a joint exposure approach that the relevance of various forms to the problem situation can be challenged. In this way the new appreciative processes can be developed.

Cultural analysis has shown that there are certain attributes in organizational life which seem to be important to the understanding of culture. It is useful to keep these in mind so that the analysis by exposure can be sought. These are listed below and are meant to act merely as a first attempt framework for anyone dealing with cultural analysis. Being open to what is going on, challenging and questioning, and always seeking to understand what seems comical to newcomers is the fundamental basis of the use of this list. The list is far from complete and likely to have considerable changes as we learn more about the nature of culture. It is to be used as a way of collecting a keener understanding of the attributes taken as being relevant by members of the culture of the problem situation. This allows for the first set of questions to be posed as the joint exposure of self-reflective learning takes place. Please do not treat this as a cookbook or menu for cultural analysis. Add to it and take from it as the learning about the situation progresses.

ATTRIBUTES OF CULTURE

HISTORY – What historical factors are taken to be held as most dear? Who are the hero figures of the past? What tales of times of stress, problems, and changes are continually retold? What values are held as vital and attributed to events with past leaders, etc.?

CONTINGENCY – What economic factors are likely to be peculiar to this setting, for example how are limited resources prioritized and valued? What factors of the incumbent society are likely to affect the values of the members? What forms of technology, if any, are dominant within this situation? What legal forms are particularly relevant to this situation?

SYMBOLIC FORMS – What verbal symbols are used in this situation but uncommon elsewhere, for example "he's a waste of rations"? What non-verbal forms are most apparent such as logos, architecture, and commonly found formal and informal behavioural idiosyncrasies? What tales, myths, legends are spoken of as being worthy of continual debate for newcomers? Listening to stories, gossip, and jokes can help to uncover what is important here.

FORMALISMS – What structures are adhered to and what history do they have? What policies are 'untouchable'? What recruitment and training procedures are taken as most important? What reward processes are operative and which are considered difficult to change?

BEHAVIOURS – What are the norms of behaviour, both formal and informal? What are the acceptable forms of personal identity? What are the conformity expectations and the limits of acceptable rebellion? Who are the key role models? What rituals and rites are performed?

Each of these attributes gives some indication of the culture of the situation. When placed together they allow for the richness of the situation to be expressed. They allow for the everyday world of the meanings of the actors in the problem situation to be exposed and explored. This allows for the structures and processes to be viewed through the eyes of those living them. These can be expressed in the form of the 'rich picture' found in soft systems methodology or in any form of representation of the situation (rich pictures are discussed in chapter 2 where an example can be found).

This discussion of culture may give the impression that cultures are consensual, have one common form and are constant. This is untrue. Although there are attributes which give an indication of constancy and consensus, cultures have subcultures, are constantly changing various aspects and forms, and often have many hidden conflicts. There are many viewpoints expressed within cultures and they often appear illogical when placed beside each other. Cultures should not be viewed as a jigsaw puzzle in which all the pieces neatly fit together, rather they are a kaleidoscope of many different forms which often conflict and seem to be in opposition to each other. Making sense of the social world is not a form of logic. Conflicts and ambiguities are to be expected in a constantly renegotiated symbolic world of interaction and change. However, one thing that can be found in cultural analysis is that there are different subcultures with radically different viewpoints. These are sometimes referred to as world views. Viewing the problem situation from these different world views is a vital part of soft systems methodology. Exposure of the different viewpoints is crucial to the gaining of an understanding of relevancy in the choice of systems models considered useful to learning.

Political analysis

In any attempt at change in a problem situation, politics will be a potential factor. Politics are endemic to the human nature. It is impossible to avoid them in any human situation so anyone who ignores them is naive in the extreme. However, some people have mastered a particular form of political art which enables them to refuse to join into the everyday politics whilst still managing to engage respect and hence to be a leader whose actions will be taken seriously. That is a very subtle form of political play. It takes a great deal of personal leadership ability to be able to carry it through. It demands understanding the politics of organizational life as does any approach to involvement in a problem situation. Any user of soft systems methodology must become involved in the situation. It is impossible to be a user without this. It follows then that any user of the methodology must seek to understand the politics of the situation. This is necessary for two reasons. First, the principles of the methodology demand analysis of the problem situation and politics are endemic to any problem situation. Second, using the methodology means involvement and that means that potentially the user is a political pawn for one or more interest groups. Self-reflection of this is necessary for survival and also in order to seek to be effective as part of that situation. Both in principle and in practice, politics are central to the methodology.

Unpacking the nature of politics in any problem situation demands some initial thought regarding categorization. It is useful to make a distinction between authority, power, and politics. These all come into play at various times and with various degrees of relative relevance. Although the situation does not actually separate them, it is helpful to treat them as separable, and in doing so to build a conceptual framework from which the situation can be viewed. This helps those within the situation to view the politically charged traps and to see which can be used helpfully and which need managing more carefully because they are reinforcing the trap.

Authority is a formal form of power which is given to individuals within situations. It is often role based and so related to the structure of the organization. For example, the Chief Executive Officer has authority because she/he has been granted that formally by being given the position as the formal leader of the organization. In a hierarchical organization, this position of authority is seen at the top of the organizational charts. In a cluster organization this authority role is seen at the centre. This form of power allocates resource-giving power to that role. This is because it allocates formal decision-making power. It is usually the most open and obvious form of power within any situation.

Power is seen in many other forms within human situations. It is often central to issues in problem situations. So what is power? There have been many attempts to define power, most of which are highly obtuse and theoretical. This is not the forum to open up and continue with that debate. A working under-standing of the concept is all that is required. Power is simply the ability to make things happen. In that manner it is a type of force, but do not be fooled into thinking that it has some form of metaphysical status which puts it above those who are influenced by it. Power is only capable of influencing and so making things happen when those in a situation allow it to be, with either self-reflective or non-reflective responses. Power is something which is attributed to people and their actions and that attribution means that others will take actions on behalf of those people with power. If no-one attributes you with power then you simply do not have it, no matter how megalomanic your interpretations of yourself are! So power is something which is attributed to individuals and is seen when they use it to influence the behaviour of others. It is also something of a commodity so it can be bestowed in various amounts. This may call to mind a situation rather like a Monty Python sketch in which someone enters a shop and asks for "two pounds of power, please", which is not quite what is meant by implying that power is given to individuals in various amounts. Amounts of power are comparative, they are also transient and difficult to understand in any quantitative form. This is especially true of the more informal power which individuals have bestowed on them or earn through actions which are held in high esteem within particular situations.

As an example, imagine a committee setting in which the siting of a new rest-room for junior executives is being discussed. The siting becomes a major desirable commodity; to win the argument regarding the siting is a major win and bestows esteem on the individual who achieves it. The committee meeting becomes a negotiating arena where each individual wishes to influence the others without being influenced themselves. They exchange their ploys whilst trying to guard against losing their influence in the exchange. It is like a game of chess where different individuals are seen as different pieces with different values and moved or sacrificed as required. Key movers emerge and it becomes more obvious that they are players rather than pieces. They have subtly negotiated what influences they have, in the form of esteem, respect, knowledge, relationships, etc. in order to gain this perception. Now the only way that the others can be sure of influencing the outcome is to back one or the other of the key movers. In doing this the individuals recognize how they can influence and decide to use that backing to support their chosen champion. This process attributes those key movers with the power-of-influence over those who have opted to see themselves as pieces on their side. The power game becomes one in which influences as commodities are gathered by getting individuals to support the various key movers. The key movers then sort themselves out as they assess their chances of winning and decide when to opt out by becoming pieces in the game and attribute their commodities of influence to other key movers. The game is one of trade-off in which the aim is to win by either being the champion or backing the champion. Nobody wants to be the key mover who ends up defeated. That gets remembered and all future power commodities lose value because of this. The outcome is that the key mover who gains the most support commodities and plays them to the best advantage and wins, and so increases the value of all those commodities. We see these kinds of scenarios every day. We have learnt to play them in kindergarten and we will still be playing them in the coach on old age pensioner outings. Gaining power and playing it is the foundation of social life.

This example highlights that power is relative to the situation but also influences other situations. It also highlights that power can be seen as some form of commodity or set of commodities which have brokerage value. Power is often valued because of historical moves and so we see history being played out as power is played out. Those who have known past champions on favourable personal bases can talk about them in special manners. This intimacy gains respect and so gains the power to influence. This is often associated with sub-groups within organizations and even with cultures and subcultures. The old boys network is where intimacy is played as a power commodity. The new guard plays a different form of intimacy as commodity. The two subcultures raise their champions who then become figure-heads who battle for the major influences in organizational change. A problem situation is likely to have many historical power transactions coming into play. It is wise to look at who is being played as champion, and who is named as having the vested power to make changes and not just the formal authoritative power. This is sometimes referred to as charisma, but charisma is only a value-laden attribution. A charismatic character is only that because those around her/him allow it. Charisma played without the consent of others looks comical and foolish no matter how strongly the individual attempts to play it. Look for the commodities of power, seek to understand in what situations those commodities have value, and seek to understand the historical nature of that value and a rudimentary understanding of power in the problem situation can be gained.

Politics are the processes whereby power commodities are formed. These processes occur continually, whether or not more constant power commodities are formed out of the process. Politicking is the manner whereby power is formed and played in order to influence the situation. To some extent politics are more visible than the exchange of power commodities. We often talk about individuals playing politics. It is this level of visibility which can render political ploys neutral and take the potential for power away from them. It is much more effective if political ploys are less visible because this makes their influence more direct and stronger. Playing power exchange locks people into a relationship where commodities are moved and favours are owed. Playing politics can make ploys visible and so weaken power commodities. If an individual decides that playing politics is the best move then she/he must be willing to take the consequences of potential loss of face and so loss of value in the power commodities. Nobody wants to be associated with the loser in an election and it can take some time for the taint of losing to wear off.

A further problem with taking the stance that individual political man-oeuvring is the best ploy is that it leads to a rather Machiavellian view of creating change in problem situations. In the liberal world which is apparently most valued today, the individual who chooses to look like a power-seeking political player who wishes to control and influence is likely to lose out. Machiavellian politics are not always a good power ploy to adopt. The situation has to be carefully read to understand this. If there is a strongly Machiavellian-type figure in the problem situation then it is worth asking why she/he is acting that way and whether that context values that style or not. It helps the process of unravelling the nature of that problem situation.

Not all political ploys are obvious. It is the subtle ploys of in-group, out-group behaviour which can be most telling. Who is allowed membership to particular decisional groups, how, and why? Who is currently in favour and who is backing them, and why? Are the champions merely puppets, manipulated by other figures who wish to remain less visible? These are questions which need addressing if a political analysis of the situation is to be made possible. A word of warning, though. Politics are both endemic and powerful. Do not fall into the trap of becoming paranoid about political ploys which are using you. Being human you will be used and you will use others; it is not necessarily occurring because someone holds something against you. For that is the viewpoint of the eternal victim. On the other hand, do not believe that because you have grasped something of the power ploys that you now have a tap on unlimited power which you can play as and when you please. This is the viewpoint of the megalomaniac. Power is contingent and those who attribute it are fickle. That is the nature of humanity and we can only act with our personal sense of ethics when seeking to understand the politics of problem situations. However, we must realize that we will be part of the politics whether we actively choose to be or not.

Having looked at the role analyses of the formal use of soft systems method-ology, and at the cultural analysis, and at the political analysis it is now possible to have some form of picture of the problem situation. This necessitates involvement in the situation and so that picture is heavily influenced by the perceptions of those involved in developing it. This is not problematical. There is no absolute true picture of any problem situation and it is the process of developing it which is most important because that is the starting point for making the traps visible. It is a vital perceptual process and this first attempt at perception needs capturing. The development of a rich picture is often noted as a useful method for capturing the picture at that time. It is simply an *aide-mémoire* to help with the comparison of systems models with this version of reality at later stages in the methodology. The rich picture should incorporate the structures and processes viewed as important by those within the situation. This allows for the climate or culture of the situation to be expressed. It gives a feel for what the situation is now and this, of itself, can be a very useful approach to starting the process of perceiving the traps so that change can occur to improve the problem situation. However, this is only calling into play the use of the concept of the appreciative system. To deal more thoroughly with the issues inherent in the situation a more formal and rigorous use of systems ideas has to be incorporated. This is the use of systems models and is discussed in the next chapters. How this use of systems ideas links into the appreciative system use of ideas needs to be expressed and that is tackled next.

Appreciation, world views, and choosing relevant systems

In this chapter, the analyses given are all guidelines for a primary development of an appreciation of the problem situation. The whole of soft systems methodology enhances that process of appreciation. It is through appreciation that change is considered, and only by appreciating the situation is it thought possible to create changes to improve the problem situation. This is discussed more thoroughly in chapter 7. Appreciation is a way of enhancing communication. However, it is unlikely that any problem situation will hold only unitary views on what that problem situation is. Because situations are developed out of communication acts which are high in ambiguity, usually there is held a plethora of different implicit models regarding what the issues are in that situation. Some of those different views will seem less transient than others and some of them will seem to be shared more readily by groups of individuals. In this way, some views are more dominant in problem situations. These views can be high in salience and so avoiding them is difficult, yet dealing with them is also difficult. The more central that views are to the values of individuals, the more they will fight to defend them. Different groups of individuals fighting for different value-laden views leads to conflict and that leads to a breakdown in communication.

Because the primary purpose of soft systems methodology is to enhance communication then this problem of value-laden views has to be understood and taken seriously. The aim is not to prove the dominance of any one view and so to try to win others over to that view but rather to tease out the different views and to show their implications on actions. This is the aim of exposure which is so central to the methodology. It is through this exposure that the traps can be seen and the consequences can be considered so that movement out of the traps can be aimed for.

Sometimes the views are intertwined with such complexity that they create whole ways of seeing the world. Everything has to fit in with the views and any conflicting information is reinterpreted so that it is meaningful in relation to those views. They literally become views of the world, that is, ways of viewing everything that is experienced. They are the frameworks by which all new experiences are judged and coded. They are so strongly internalized that any attempt to expose them is treated with contempt, abuse, or simply distrust. This makes the job of exposure extremely difficult and dangerous.

Although individuals hold these world views, they are developed out of social interactions. These views are often contingent upon the situation even though strongly guarded by individuals. By viewing them as central to the situation they can be approached as less threatening than by viewing them as central to the individuals. It is then that the situation has to be seen to be changed rather than the individuals. Transference of the siting of these world views is not just for convenience. They have emerged out of situational issues. It is revealing to see individuals who are considered terrors at work play gently and caringly with their children at home. They perceive that the situations are different and feel happy with radically different forms of behaviour in the two situations. To get cooperation out of the individual whilst at work may demand changing the situation so that it is more attributable with the forms of action that are perceived to be important in the home life. In that way an individual who is incongruent with the aims of the workplace can gain congruency by reassessing the views held regarding the workplace. The situation can be changed because it is no longer seen as an inevitable trap and so the actions used in another situation can be imported to improve that situation. The critical question to be addressed is "Why is the work situation incongruent at present?" The dominant world views need to be explored to try and answer this.

Using the analyses discussed throughout this chapter, different dominant world views can be uncovered. These are the world views which are inherent to that situation. This is different from world views which are relevant to learning about that situation. In a situation it may be that dominant world views are held regarding the use of resources. People see themselves as resources to support work activities or as labour commodities to be abused by those in charge. These are two dominant and opposing world views of the same actions regarding the use of human resources for work. People can fit many different sets of actions and circumstances, into an explanation of events, when seeking to prove the truth value of their viewpoint. This leads to opposition and conflict. Two viewpoints become so intertwined in the everyday lives of the individuals in the situation that they do not recognize them as two viewpoints. They are taking them for granted. Exposing them as viewpoints can be useful because they do not realize how effective these are in influencing their daily lives. This is using the viewpoints inherent in the situation as being relevant to learning about the situation. In using soft systems methodology, they would be named as relevant systems, that is, systems relevant to learning about the problem situation. They could be named as a "human resource managing system" and a "labour commodity exploiting system", and the corresponding actions and consequences of each discussed. There is, however, an alternative generation of relevant systems.

Any naming of systems, which is likely to help support the learning process of appreciating the problem situation, is relevant. It is unlikely that there will be any irrelevant systems because learning can be teased out of any metaphor! However, for the purposes of time management it may be worthwhile to attempt to name relevant systems which are more obviously relevant to learning. These can be generated from uncovering the different world views dominant in the situation. They can quite easily come from other sources. For example, in looking at work and human resource issues it could be useful to name a "work allocating system" as relevant. Asking questions about owners and customers in the CATWOE consideration can be enlightening. It may also be less direct, and so less threatening, than using the more obvious systems first named. Anything which helps the process of debate is useful in considering the naming of relevant systems. This means that, although any named system is potentially relevant, naming it is not a trivial task. Naming relevant systems has to consider the political impact of exposure and whether it is good to expose certain opposing viewpoints immediately and directly, or whether a middle ground discussion would not be more useful. Any user of the methodology, and that may be a group of those within the situation, is part of the political process and must consider the political consequences of all aspects of using the methodology. This is particularly apparent when the choosing of relevant systems is considered.

When choosing relevant systems there is one thing that must be kept in mind. There is a tendency for people to become enamoured of their models, having spent much time and effort developing them. This has to be avoided. The models are merely a means to encourage debate. One way of actively seeking to avoid this issue is to generate many models at once. Generating many models in parallel can be a daunting task for the newly initiated so is not necessarily recommended for a novice! However, the generation of many named relevant systems is less awesome. Those in the situation should be encouraged to use the process of naming of relevant systems to open up the debate. The generation of many alternatives can lead to the questioning of relevance and that can uncover and expose traps. Seeing the world of traps is the crucial aspect of the methodology and every opportunity to do this is worthwhile. However, there is one note of caution. Relevant systems are first named in the real world set of actions. It is here that transition into the world of systems thinking occurs. It is crucial that the transition occurs, or the world of politics and conflict can become the central arena of the debate and can lock-in the debate so that progress is limited. The models provide a metaphorical distancing from this political arena. Their development needs to be treated as important to the overall process of learning-by-using-the-methodology. Getting out of the political arena and into modelling is important if systems thinking is going to be used adequately rather than assumed to be used and treated intuitively. Generate many named relevant systems, and discuss them, but move on to modelling.

This chapter has dealt with the first analyses in soft systems methodology, that is, the analyses of the problem situation. This is essentially open, and so can be returned to as often as is seen to be desirable. The concepts of the trap, the appreciative setting, roles, culture, and politics are all fundamental to the concept of the problem situation as discussed here. Their consideration provides the basis for the use of systems thinking to enhance the debate and so to help achieve improvement of the problem situation.

Discussion issues

1. Discuss how information can be used politically.

2. Discuss the dominant world views which you think are present in your current working situation. How are conflicts of opinions dealt with?

3. Discuss the possible roles, values, and norms attached to being an information manager.

Exercises

Appreciating human situations as problem situations is the central theme to this chapter. This appreciation can carry on indefinitely. However, to formalize it more the following exercises should help.

1. In your current work situation, look for the different views expressed. Can you find evidence of just two views which are strongly supported? Do they appear to be in opposition? Try to name these views in systems terms, that is, as systems which do something ("a house destroying system", or "a site clearing system", or "a rubbish creating system", or "a scrap making system" – notice that there is a noun, followed by a verb with -ing at the end, followed by the term system. This is a useful guideline to naming systems as human activity systems).

2. Taking those views can you find anything which people constantly express which seems to be a metaphor rather than just a naming of something in relation to those views? Examples are "it's my baby" or "he's a real warrior" or "let's run with this one" or "we are being ripped off". These are often value statements. Can you find clusters of these expressed values which give an indication of a common theme? Try to gather these by listening at coffee breaks when people are gossiping. It can be very revealing.

3. Go back to the Army study in chapter two and analyze the roles, values, and norms presented there. What political exchanges could have been going on?

4. From any of the situations you have been looking at, try to develop a rich picture whilst working either alone or with others from that situation. Look for important structures in the situation and in the conflicts. Look for communication structures. Look for the processes of conflict and try to express how they are occurring. Express the key figures in pictorial form. Avoid language and avoid too many arrows. This is not a systems description but a pictorial description. Draw people rather than things. You are trying to express a problem situation which has been created by human actions. What have you learnt about the problem situation from doing this? Did you learn more by discussing it as a member of a group or by working alone? If you worked alone, how transferable do you think your picture is to those within the situation?

These exercises will help you get a feel for problem situations. That is the basis of the methodology and helps you use modelling effectively.

Suggested reading

Checkland, P.B. and Scholes, J., *Soft Systems Methodology in Action*, Wiley, Chichester, UK, 1990.

> This provides a thorough discussion of the up-to-date thinking regarding soft systems methodology. It gets away from merely viewing it as a seven-stage model and deals more with what it is to use the methodology. It is particularly useful in supporting this chapter as it deals with the different forms of analysis which have been covered here.

Vickers, G., Sir, *Human Systems are Different*, Open University Press, Milton Keynes, UK, 1983.

> This is a collection of writings published posthumously following Sir Geoffrey's death in 1981. They are extremely lucid writings, full of insight on the nature of human systems, particularly dealing with the process of appreciation and the effect of the trap on decision-making.

Part II

Soft systems modelling

The next three chapters take the reader on a detailed learning journey through the technical aspects of rigorously using systems ideas to investigate problem situations. The first two chapters do not concern themselves with the real world of social events but, instead, concentrate on developing defensible soft systems models. Chapter 4 looks at relevant systems and root definitions, giving guidance, examples, and exercises to the reader so that these technical aspects can be learnt. Chapter 5 builds upon that by taking the reader through the same process whilst looking at conceptual model building. Chapter 6, the final in this section, deals with the comparison process where the models are taken back to the social world so that learning may occur. This is done in a variety of forms which differ in their formality of approach. These three chapters give a more detailed approach to the development of soft systems modelling than is currently available in any other book.

Because there is so little available material in book form which provides education on how to conduct the technicalities of modelling correctly, the readings are not given at the end of each chapter. Instead, the suggested readings to cover all chapters in this section are given below.

Suggested readings

1. Checkland, P.B., *Systems thinking, systems practice*, Wiley, Chichester, 1981.

2. Checkland, P.B., & Scholes, J., *Soft systems methodology in action*, Wiley, Chichester, 1990.

4 Modelling human activity systems: root definitions of relevant systems

- *Modelling in soft systems methodology*
- *Generating relevant systems*
- *Primary-task systems*
- *Issue-based systems*
- *'Service' versus 'non-service' systems*
- *A typology of relevant systems*
- *Naming systems in root definitions*
- *The CATWOE concept*
- *Root definitions*

Chapters 4, 5 and 6 cover the core technical activities involved in soft systems methodology that are concerned with generating and using models of human activity systems. This chapter focuses upon the methods and techniques involved in the first stage of generating systems models, and is concerned with the process of formally describing an activity system in the form of a root definition. The aim of this chapter is to provide a guide to producing root definitions which are both,

    a) potentially relevant to the problem situation, and

    b) rigorously expressed.

The steps involved in generating root definitions are the identification of relevant systems and the formulation of formal system names in the form of root definitions. In terms of the methodology this chapter corresponds to concepts 3 and 3a of figure 4.1. The areas covered are the formulation of root definitions of relevant systems and the use of the CATWOE concept to ensure that the root definitions are well structured and well expressed.

The formal naming of a system is the first major step in generating a model of a human activity system. It is in this process that the step across from the real world to the systems thinking world is made. In other words the move is made from concentrating upon the richness and complexity of the problem situation which has been uncovered in the opening stages of soft systems methodology towards the creation of rigorously derived systems models, which express how a set of activities to carry out some action pertinent to the situation would ideally be organized.

The processes involved in the whole of systems modelling are:
1. Generating relevant systems
2. Naming the system as a root definition.
3. Transforming the root definition into a conceptual model.
4. Comparing the model with the situation.

The first two processes will be discussed in this chapter and the various methods and techniques for carrying out the activities involved in the processes will be described.

Modelling in soft systems methodology

In soft systems methodology (see figure 4.1), models of human activity systems are produced which provide a potentially useful framework against which actions carried out within the problem situation can be compared. In this way a deeper understanding of those actions may be developed. The models are not descriptions of the actions in the situation but are rather an expression of the concept of a human activity system. Such models express the idea of the ideally organized set of activities required in order to achieve a specified purpose.

In real situations actions are often very complex and concerned with achieving many things simultaneously. Such activities can be very difficult to understand in totality, therefore models are used which provide a means of focusing on particular aspects of the situation. The aim of modelling is therefore to provide a simple, coherent, and defensible representation of an organized set of activities such that it is relevant to understanding some of the complexity of the real world action. Models of human activity systems must therefore represent the minimum, but necessary, set of activities which would be required to achieve some purpose in an organized (systemic) way. These considerations mean that modelling has to take into account a number of factors:

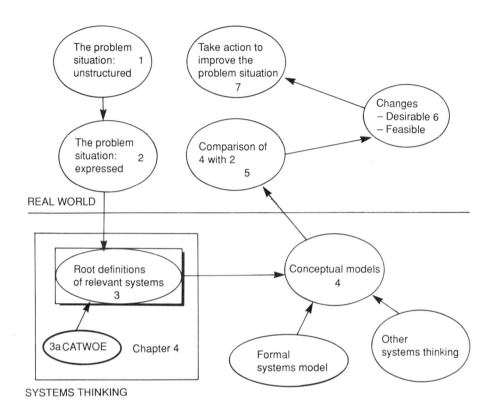

Figure 4.1   Soft systems methodology

1. The model should represent no more, but no less, than the activities required
    to achieve the purpose in a systemic manner.
    If it represented more than required then the model could be challenged as
    inefficient, whereas if it contained less than the required activities it could
    be challenged as being inoperable.
2. The model should meet the criteria for being a system.
    Systems theory is concerned with the idea of organization and provides, in
    the form of the open systems model, the elements of what is involved in
    being well organized. Therefore a systems model should represent an ideal
    form of being well organized for the particular purpose specified. Only by
    ensuring that our models meet the criteria for being systems can we be sure
    that they represent the ideal form of being organized.

3. Modelling should be rigorous and defensible.

    Hopefully when a model has been created, it will be used in a comparison process out of which will come ideas for changes to the situation. The defensibility of the proposed changes depends in part on how well the modelling process has been carried out. The defensibility of the model and hence of the proposed changes rests upon the first two criteria. This in turn means that the whole modelling process must be open to inspection and that each stage of the process must be documented so that it can be evaluated against the principles of good modelling practice that have been developed and which are presented in this chapter.

4. Modelling should be flexible.

    There may be many models which are relevant in any given situation and therefore the process must allow for the development of many models, and not seek to restrict the choice of model to some idea of the best model.

In this chapter the stages of the modelling process are discussed and illustrated in order to provide the reader with a sound basis upon which to develop modelling skills. Developing models is a skill, and therefore the reader is encouraged to practice the skill at every opportunity.

Generating relevant systems

In any situation there will be many ways of looking at what is going on, at what the problems are and so on. Exploring these different ways of looking at the situation may prove very useful in tackling the problem of bringing about change and improvement. The process of expressing the situation, which was discussed in chapter 3, should have provided many ideas about what, in systems terms, might be useful to explore. In writing this text, for example, we might be interested in a 'writing system', or a 'reader informing system', or a 'keeping the publisher happy system', or a 'disturbance reducing system', and many more.

Take for example a company that produces and sells motor cars. It could be seen as a 'manufacturing system', a 'providing goods to a market for a profit system', 'a system to develop and market the latest motor car technology', 'a system to provide cheap, readily available, personal transport', 'a system to create machines to turn valuable non-renewable sources of energy into gaseous pollutants', 'a system to manage assets provided by shareholder investment in such a manner that by the creation and sale of motor cars it generates surplus income which can be distributed back to the shareholders as a return upon their investment', 'a system which provides employment to a group of people', or 'a system which provides an interesting and fulfilling working environment'. The list of potential ways of looking at the company is limited, in principle at least, only by the imagination. Each view might provide different insights into the company and thus help us to learn about the company which in turn should provide a deeper understanding of it.

At this point, the aim within soft systems methodology (SSM) is to generate a rich list of would-be relevant systems. A list from which some of the relevant systems can be chosen for further refinement into human activity system models. Generating a long list of relevant systems should not be a problem in itself, but in practice it often seems to be. The major cause of this difficulty is concentrating too hard on the notion of relevance. A system is relevant to the extent that it can lead to insight into the situation, suggest possible changes, and generally aids the problem-solving effort. However the paradox is that there is no way of telling whether a system is relevant until it has been formally modelled and used in a comparison process. It would be better to regard ideas for systems, at this stage, as might-be relevant systems. The general rule is not to discard anything, indeed to collect as many ideas as possible.

It has been found useful to use creativity techniques, such as brainstorming, to aid the generation of relevant systems. A slightly more structured approach is the use of similes and metaphors. For example the question might be posed "If this organization were a motor car what type would it be?" Is it a sports model, an old banger, a family saloon, a classic, a Rolls-Royce? This can then be elaborated further by looking at the various roles associated with motor cars, e.g. the driver, a passenger, a mechanic, or a salesman, and at what problems they might have. Essentially, the situation is being looked at from a more familiar perspective and in a language which is ready made for expressing aspects of the situation. A sales department might be regarded as a sports car requiring fast reactions and good road sense to drive, needing passengers with good nerves, but probably needing specialized mechanics to maintain it as well as being expensive on fuel. On the other hand an administration department might be regarded as an old banger; cheap to run, easy to drive if a bit slow, and in need of constant but simple attention, however, it may break down at a crucial moment. Each image thus generated provides opportunities for recognizing might-be relevant systems.

Although there is no way of guaranteeing that a particular might-be relevant system will turn out to be actually relevant, in advance of formal modelling and comparison it has been found useful to consider different types of relevant systems. There are four types of relevant system: primary-task, issue-based, service, and non-service systems.

Primary-task systems

Many organizations, and other forms of organized activity, are set up explicitly to carry out some stated task. A primary-task approach is concerned with trying to create systems relevant to exploring this aspect of the situation. The aim is to express a would-be neutral account of the primary-task activities. Thus, considering the Ford Motor Company to be a manufacturing system, or a car producing system would be to take a primary-task approach.

Two methods for generating primary-task systems have been developed, the first takes some public account of the activity as the basis for a system, whilst the second seeks to develop an expression of the activity which is acceptable to all the parties concerned with the situation.

Often organizations try to present some public account of what they are about. This may take the form of a mission statement, or a charter, which can be found in the official publications of the organization. It is normally relatively easy to convert such statements into formal systems definitions and hence to model the implied human activity system.

The second approach is to seek agreement amongst the problem owners in the situation upon the wording of the root definition. This implies creating an interactive process whereby the participants contribute to the wording of the root definition. This may be achieved by holding workshops in which the development of a statement about the organization is the focus of activity. In such cases, care must be taken to explain the reasons for building a model in this way and the technicalities of the language (CATWOE etc.) demonstrated. The advantage of operating in this manner is that the process focuses attention upon the nature of the activities involved in the organization and that commitment to a definition is facilitated. This in turn helps to create commitment to the other activities involved in soft systems methodology and in particular to the lessons and issues which arise from the later comparison process.

Particularly with primary-task models, it is to be expected that such models actually reflect the actions undertaken by the organization and it is therefore to be expected that at the comparison stage, evidence will be found to support the idea that the organization actually does carry out the activities generated in the model. It is therefore possible to regard the comparison stage as a means of validating the model. Validated primary-task models are extremely useful as they represent an organized representation of the core activities of the organization. They can therefore be used as a firm basis upon which to tackle issues with respect to secondary activities, such as the provision of information, where such activities are services provided in support of the core activities.

Issue-based systems

An alternate form of relevance type is to consider the issues or problems evident in a situation, and to base the generation of relevant systems upon these. These are termed issue-based systems.

It might be evident, for example, that in a situation there is a great deal of animosity and conflict between certain problem owners, or groups of problem owners. It might be relevant to consider both a 'conflict-reducing system' and a 'conflict-generating system' as worthy of further investigation.

Issue-based systems are somewhat different to primary-task ones in that it is less likely that they will be represented in a situation as fully as primary-task activities. In the example above it would not be expected that a conflict-reducing system would exist in the situation, and although conflict generation is evident it is unlikely that this operates in a formal and organized manner. Developing and using systems models of this sort can provide great insight into a situation and it might be possible to think through the problems of creating a conflict-reducing mechanism through the use of such a model.

'Service' versus 'non-service' systems

The distinction between these two types of system has been developed out of the experience of modelling various types of systems. This experience has been encoded into the law of conceptualization (Checkland 1981, page 237), which states: "... a system which serves another system cannot be defined and modelled until a definition and a model of the system served are available."

A system to organize and manage the information required for the functioning of another system is a service system. A root definition and conceptual model of such a system must of necessity take into account the nature of the system which is served; if it does not then the model generated will be rather general, and is unlikely to prove of use in the analysis of a situation. It is, therefore, necessary to model the non-service system before moving to the service system.

A typology of relevant systems

It has been explained earlier that identifying truly relevant systems is not possible without having defined, modelled, and compared them. The search for relevance is indeed part of the process of iteration through the activities of soft systems methodology. It is not possible, therefore, to present guidelines for the choice of relevant systems as such, but it is possible to combine the types of relevant systems discussed above into a framework which is useful for managing the process. The most general guidance for generating relevant systems is to consider as wide a variety of options as possible. However, in practice users tend to choose one system which seems sensible and then shy away from considering alternatives. The use of the typology of relevant systems at least helps to ensure that the search for relevant systems is kept open to a reasonable degree. See figure 4.2 below.

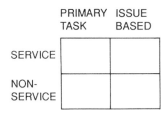

Figure 4.2 The typology of relevant systems

Having generated a list of would-be relevant systems, then these should be classified according to the sectors of the typology above. Any further generation of relevant systems should concentrate upon those in any under-represented sector until there are a reasonably equal number of entries in each sector. As a rule-of-thumb it is good practice on a first pass of this activity to generate at least five different entries for each sector of the typology. At least one relevant system from each sector should then be chosen for subsequent modelling.

The aim of generating relevant systems, and of subsequently modelling them, is to focus in an organized way upon some area of the situation which may provide some insight into the problems and issues towards which the study is directed. The analyses covered in chapter 3 should have provided a rich insight into the problems of the situation and it is useful to try to relate the relevant systems under consideration to the problems and issues which have been identified. A list should be prepared of problem areas together with relevant systems which might help focus upon those problems. Thus:

PROBLEM AREA	RELEVANT SYSTEM	COMMENT
1. ---------	1. ------------	why it
	2. ------------	might be
2. ---------	3. ------------	useful to
	4. ------------	use this
	5. ------------	system.
	6. ------------	

This list is used in a number of ways, firstly to help organize the choice of relevant systems to be modelled, and secondly to help evaluate the results of using the model in the comparison process. The comparison process is covered in more detail in chapter 6. It is usual to find that new problem areas will be uncovered and that some areas, which it was thought might be tackled using a particular relevant system, were not covered by that system. The listing of problem areas and relevant systems thus provides a good way of recording and managing the results of the systems modelling and comparison processes involved in soft systems methodology, and in turn it allows for the cycles of modelling activity in a study to be managed in a coherent way.

Thus together, the typology of relevant systems and the matching of problem areas to relevant systems provides a firm foundation both for the subsequent stages of the methodology and for the management of the whole process of problem-tackling.

Naming systems in root definitions

Having chosen a relevant system, it is then necessary to formalize this idea into a more substantial concept of a system. This formalization is done in two stages: firstly the system is carefully named in a root definition, and then the minimum but necessary activities to be the system named in the root definition are assembled and structured into a conceptual model. The root definition and conceptual model thus form a mutually supportive pair. The root definition provides the foundation for the model and the model represents the root definition. It follows therefore that sound conceptual models are built upon the basis of sound, well-thought out, and well-developed root definitions.

The basic form of a root definition is:

A system

: to do X

: by means of Y

: in order to achieve Z.

At this point it is necessary to consider in more detail the various parts of this statement. The most important part is the term system.

In the sense used within soft systems methodology a system is the general concept of an organized whole.

1. The organized whole consists of parts or components connected together in an organized way.

2. The parts are affected by being in the system and changed if they leave it.

3. The assembly of parts DOES something, more formally defined as transforming some input into an output.

4. The system is a concept developed by, used by, and thought to be meaningful by a human being.

This idea of system is summarized in figure 4.3.

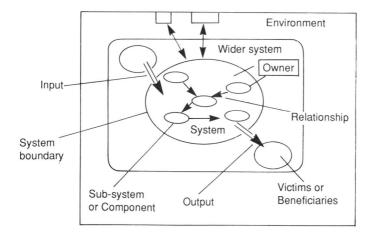

Figure 4.3 The concept of system

The aim in developing a root definition is to capture the major elements involved in the system. For human activity systems the major elements involved have been formalized into the mnemonic CATWOE. The CATWOE concept was originally developed as a means of analyzing root definitions and identifying weaknesses in their structure; however it has also been found in practice to be extremely valuable as an aid to creating root definitions.

The CATWOE concept

The main elements of a well formulated root definition have been found to be Customers, Actors, Transformation, Weltanschauung, Owner, and Environment, hence the mnemonic CATWOE. The terms are derived from a consideration of the system concepts shown above as expressed in a language appropriate to human activity systems. Each of these terms will now be discussed in more detail.

Customers

Customers are those people, or other activity systems, who are the direct victims or beneficiaries of the system being developed. They are those people or systems associated with the inputs and outputs of the system.

Actors

An actor is a person who carries out one or more of the activities in the system. This can be particularly important when dealing with a system which would require a specific type of actor, e.g. a doctor, if it were to be made operational.

The concept of actor can be extended to some extent to cover other resources which are vital to the operability of a particular system. In such cases it would be essential to include in the activity model created from the root definition activities which ensured the adequate supply of these vital resources to the activity system, as a loss of such resources would lead to the operational failure of the system.

Transformation

The fundamental concept of an activity system is that it converts some input into some output. This conversion process is termed the transformation and it is of vital importance. In SSM the interest is focused upon purposeful action, that is, organized action which brings about some change in the world. Therefore, in creating the concept of a system relevant to such action, the idea of change and hence the concept of transformation is of central concern. Indeed, without a transformation it would not be possible to create a human activity system, which is after all the purpose of systems modelling.

The transformation in a root definition should be singular and logically coherent. It is often tempting to put more than one transformation into a root definition but this leads to difficulties in creating conceptual models. In such circumstances it is better to create two root definitions and two models and then consider the need to amalgamate them. Any real world purposeful activity can be seen in many different ways and hence as performing many different transformations. The aim of modelling is to unpack this complexity and set out the particular views in isolation. It is, therefore, a sound principle to keep a root definition as simple as possible and the main aspect of this simplification is to use only one transformation in a root definition.

The principle of logical coherence is fundamental to good systems modelling. If it is logically impossible to convert the input into the output then the stated transformation is impossible, and hence a valid activity model cannot be generated from the particular root definition. It is logically possible to transform raw materials into finished goods, and it is logically possible to transform materials of one level of value into materials of another level of value. However the transformation of raw materials into profit is not logically coherent. Raw materials are tangible physical objects whereas profit is an abstract measure of the difference between income and expenditure. It is not possible to transform a physical object logically into an abstract measurement and therefore such a transformation would be logically incoherent. In the case of profit it might be better to regard this as a measure of performance of carrying out a transformation process rather than as a direct transformation in its own right.

The need for logical coherence is vital in a transformation statement and therefore it is good practice to set out the input and output of the transformation and check that these are of the same logical type, e.g. physical object to physical object, level of attribute to level of attribute, etc.

Weltanschauung

Weltanschauung (or 'W' for short) is that image of the world which makes the human activity system being defined meaningful. Again it must be repeated that an activity model is an ideal representation of one particular view of some purposeful action. If such a representation is to have any meaning or significance then it must be related to those ways of thinking about the world which imply that significance. A model is a simplification, which in this context means that some aspects of the world have been taken for granted. Therefore the model is only of value in relation to these assumptions which are made about the world.

People make sense of the world through creating images of it. Images which are created through experience and communicated through interaction with others. Images which are so familiar that they are taken for granted and go often unquestioned. It is these unquestioned images and assumptions which may need to be brought to the surface and examined to some degree as part of the problem-solving process.

When a relevant system is generated and a root definition written, assumptions and taken-for-granted aspects of the world are inevitably embedded into the root definition. These aspects are the Weltanschauung of the model.

Bringing into focus the Weltanschauung of a model by use of the CATWOE concept can be a very insightful part of the enquiry process created by using SSM. It also means that models which regard the situation from very different Ws may be generated and modelled, and thus contrasting views of a situation may be utilized within SSM.

In practice it is quite difficult to write down an explicit W statement and then incorporate it explicitly into a root definition, but it is very useful to consider a range of different Ws for any relevant system and then create very different root definitions. It is much easier to use the W concept in the analysis role for which it was first intended. In this mode the root definition is created and then the question of the W which makes the definition meaningful is addressed. Creating a conceptual model involves assembling and structuring the minimum but necessary set of activities required to be the system named in the root definition, and a sound understanding of the W implicit within a root definition is of considerable value in carrying out this process.

Owner

The owner of the system is that person, system or agency which has the power to direct and ultimately abolish the system under consideration. In many situations it is relatively easy to identify the owner element, for example a board of directors of a company, but in others this might be a diverse and informal set of owners who could through agreement abolish the system.

Environment

There will inevitably be elements outside of the system under consideration which have to be taken as given. In many circumstances these elements may impose constraints upon the form of activity that is possible. These are referred to as environmental constraints. For example, consider a manufacturing system which transforms raw materials into finished goods. In the environment of such a system will be the raw material suppliers, the suppliers of resources to the activity system, and the disseminators of the finished goods. In a particular root definition it may be necessary to take these elements as given and consider the relationships and constraints that these elements impose upon the activity system.

It is not necessary that all of the CATWOE elements are filled in any given root definition, but as a minimum there must be a logically coherent transformation and a Weltanschauung. If there were no transformation then the definition would not be a system, and in any statement there will always be an implied Weltanschauung. The other CATWOE elements should have been considered and a deliberate decision made whether or not to incorporate them into the root definition. They should not be ignored by default.

Again it is necessary to emphasize the point that the system model is an ideal concept. This means that the choice of CATWOE elements is the responsibility of the modeller. Perhaps, because of this, the term candidate element should be used, e.g. who are candidates for the role of customer, actor, owner and environmental element. By being able to generate different root definitions and models it is possible to explore the consequences of choosing certain candidates to fill the available roles. For example, consider a manufacturing system, it would be quite natural to regard the owner of such a system as the board of directors, but if the workers withdrew their labour then the system could be abolished, so too if the suppliers refused to supply, yet the board, workers and suppliers may well have different ideas of what good performance from the system might be. It is legitimate, within activity system modelling, to define these different owners and produce models which reflect their different concerns and thus explore the real situation from these differing perspectives.

It is a useful practice to generate and record the many possible candidates for a particular role using the CATWOE concept. This in turn helps generate ideas for future relevant systems and allows for the organized generation of variations upon the theme of a particular relevant system.

A general format for a root definition, following Checkland (1981, page 317), which takes account of the CATWOE elements is:

"An 'O'-owned system which, under the environmental constraints 'E' which it takes as given, transforms 'Input' into 'Output' by carrying out the activities of '............' amongst others. The transformation is carried out by 'A' and will affect 'C'. The system is made meaningful by a view of the world captured in 'W'".

Root definitions: development guidelines

A root definition is the first stage in the process of formalizing ideas about a human activity system which will eventually end in the development of an activity system model. It is both an aid to modelling and a necessary constraint upon it. The most important part of the root definition is the transformation and this should be the starting point for development.

Consider the writing of this book, a relevant system might be concerned with taking in the ideas, concepts and approaches which form SSM and presenting them in a way accessible to a particular audience. Thus the transformation of the system would be to take ideas and concepts which are published in a wide range of documents (the input) and convert them into an appropriately presented set of ideas and concepts (the output).

Having captured the transformation and confirmed that it is logically acceptable, then the root definition can be developed further. SSM modelling is concerned with activities and hence uses the verbs of the English language as the modelling elements, as will be discussed in the next section. It is therefore useful to incorporate a reasonable number of verbs into the root definition as part of the means to achieve the transformation.

Thus we have 'A system to convert ideas and concepts structured in one way into ideas and concepts structured in another way by capturing, organizing and presenting them'.

This provides the basis around which the other elements of the root definition can be built.

Consider the other CATWOE elements:

Customer: the victims or beneficiaries of this system would be the audience. It would be possible to consider at least four types of audience: academic, student, practitioner, and mixed. Each audience would lead to different modes of presentation being most applicable.

Actors: the activities in the system would be carried out by the authors, although other actors such as the publisher's editor might become involved in some aspects of the system.

Transformation: ideas in format A $\Longrightarrow$ T $\Longrightarrow$ ideas in format B

Weltanschauung: The question here is why one would want to carry out this activity and what makes it a sensible thing to do. Two aspects are important. Firstly there must be a belief that the ideas, concepts and methods which form SSM are of interest and value to the audience, and secondly that the presentation structure presently available is inappropriate for the audience concerned. If either of these were not the case then the activity would become empty.

Owner: There are two main candidates for ownership. The authors may be regarded as the owners but also the publisher might also be regarded as such. The owners' aspirations for the system are important in determining the form of system performance measures that one might see as applicable to the system and therefore such a choice would lead to some differences of detail in an activity model. For the purposes of exposition a generalized owner will be taken so that at the stages of modelling and comparison the aspect of choosing different ownership may be explored.

Environmental constraints: What must the system take as given?

The system is not concerned to change or develop ideas and concepts, therefore it must take these as given.

The actors have other commitments for their time, and there is a limited supply of other resources. The system is not concerned with generating resources, and it therefore must operate within the constraint of available resources.

Our intention is to produce a book which means that the mode of presentation is limited. The form, size, and general format of the book are given by the publisher and these are constraints within which the system must work.

Having thought through the various elements of the root definition it is now possible to state it in its fully-fledged form.

It is **an owner-owned system, manned and operated by authors which seeks to capture, organize and present the ideas, concepts and approach which form soft systems methodology in a form more appropriate to an audience than the form in which these ideas and concepts are currently encountered. The system takes as given the nature of the ideas and concepts, which are regarded as valuable both academically and practically but which** are not easily available to the audience. **The system must operate within the resource constraints created by the wider situation of the authors and within the technical constraints of the mode of presentation and the publisher.**

You should now analyze this root definition using the CATWOE concept to check that it coincides with the one given above. The term 'seeks' has been introduced to indicate that the system cannot definitively know in advance that its new mode of presentation will be acceptable to the audience, rather the system must learn its way to an acceptable outcome. The customer has been linked into the transformation to create the idea of a form more appropriate, which in turn provides a means for the system to evaluate its progress by defining a more appropriate form of presentation, and then seeking to create this.

Throughout the development of the root definition the terms have become more focused and the ideas clearer, but they have gradually moved further away from what is actually happening in the real world situation. The root definition focuses the thinking and each word within it is carefully chosen and plays an important part, but the development process has also created many more ideas for root definitions, and of course one is always at liberty to return to a prior stage and choose a different root definition.

However, having gone this far, the stage is set for the last step in the modelling process, which is to create an activity model from the root definition. An activity model which encapsulates all the thinking about this particular relevant system, which is logically coherent, and has the minimum but necessary activities to be the system named in the root definition. It is this final step, activity system modelling, to which attention is given in chapter 5. The remainder of this chapter will cover more examples of generating well-formulated root definitions.

Root definitions: The Floppit Corporation

Consider the following, the managing director of the Floppit Corporation has requested that you carry out a systems study of the corporation as an aid to managing its future development. A preliminary study of the background to the corporation has been completed using the analyses 1, 2 and 3 as were discussed in chapter 3. The time has come to think about the study and how it should progress. The situation is outlined in figure 4.4 below.

Looking at the situation, there are two areas of concern which arise from thinking in terms of the basic model of a study situation. Firstly, how should the study be organized and secondly how should the Floppit Corporation be viewed and analyzed. Thus we can think in terms of systems models which are relevant to the study situation and its problems, as well as systems models which are relevant to the Floppit Corporation and its problems. It is useful to apply the typology of relevant systems to each area and attempt to generate a range of relevant systems for the situation.

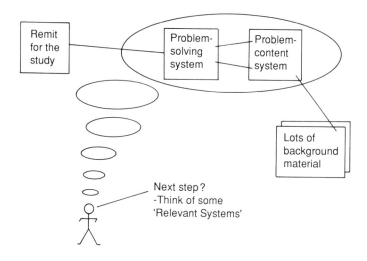

Figure 4.4 The Floppit Corporation study

At this point in any study it is difficult to know what to look at, what to concentrate upon, and hence what information is required to proceed further. It is the aim of generating and using systems models to provide a coherent framework which allows us to focus upon certain areas in an organized and controlled way. Let us follow the process through and generate some relevant systems. The problem-solving system and problem-content system are linked together as the diagram shows but only by breaking into these relationships and thinking about the whole situation in an organized way can progress be made.

[Exercise

Generate a set of relevant systems for the Floppit Corporation situation, before reading the remainder of this section.]

Relevant systems
The problem solving system
Primary-task (non-service)

1. A system to carry out a soft systems study relevant to organizational development
2. A problem generating system
3. A solution generating system
4. A results transferring system
5. A change generating system.

Issue-based (non-service)

1. A system-study approach choosing system
2. A resource acquiring system
3. A progress reporting system
4. A system maintaining access to the right people
5. An egg-on-the-face-avoiding system.

Primary-task (service)
[in a service system consideration must be given to the system being served]

1. An organizational development process aiding system –
      the organizational development process
2. An MD helping system – the MD
3. An organization learning facilitating system – the organization
4. A system to aid management problem-solving –
      the management problem-solving process.

Issue-based (service)

1. A system to contribute to systems learning –
      the systems learning community
2. An organizational conflict reducing system –
      the organizational conflict process

3. A system to provide an acceptable working environment for project members – the nature of the working environment.
4. An organizational-power acquiring system –
    the nature of power in the organization.

This list provides many different ways of looking at the study and its associated project. Choosing a particular relevant system for further modelling will enable us to concentrate in more detail upon that particular area in a controlled way. The second area for consideration is the content of the organizational situation.

The problem content system
Primary-task (non-service)
   1. A floppit manufacturing system
   2. A system to make and sell floppits
   3. A system to add value to a set of raw materials by converting them into a saleable product known as a floppit.

Issue-based (non-service)
   1. A new product generating system
   2. A finance managing system
   3. A people managing system
   4. A system to provide a working environment which is both conducive to productivity and fulfilling to the staff involved
   5. A departmental budgeting system.

Primary-task (service)
   1. A need-for-floppits market-fulfilling system – the floppits market
   2. A return-on-investment generating system
   3. A profit generating system
   4. A financial surplus generating system.

Issue-based (non-service)
   1. A shareholder confidence maintaining system – the shareholders
   2. An investment generating system – the investment marketplace

   3. A finance controlling system – the financial transactions of the
      corporation
   4. A management informing system – the management structure
   5. A production controlling system – the production system.

Once an initial list of relevant systems has been generated, attention can then
be directed towards the systems modelling process. The process of formalizing
a relevant system into a root definition, which has been described earlier, can
now be undertaken. The process is the same for whatever type of relevant system
that is being dealt with, except where a relevant system is being treated as a
service system, and it is necessary to define and model the system being served
prior to formulating the desired root definition.

[1. How did your relevant systems compare with the examples given above?
You will probably find that your primary-task systems were close to the
examples above, but that your issue-based systems were different.
Remember that the list given is a set of examples, and not a definitive answer.
Hopefully you generated many more than we did – Good!

2. Now choose one primary-task and one issue-based relevant system for the
problem solving system, and one of each for the problem content system.
Prepare a root definition and CATWOE analysis for each relevant system (four
in all). Do this before reading the next sections.]

Root definitions

A few examples of root definitions derived from the relevant systems generated
above will now be given. The form of the root definition is the same whichever
type of relevant system is chosen. This does not mean that the effort of
generating different types of relevant system is wasted, because the type of
system will be used again when the comparison process is reached in stage 5 of
soft systems methodology (see chapter 6). The examples given are:
   1. A system to carry out a soft systems study
   2. A progress reporting system
   3. A floppit manufacturing and selling system
   4. A system to provide a working environment which is both conducive to
      productivity and fulfilling to the staff involved.

Example 1. A system to carry out a soft systems study

This relevant system is associated with the problem solving system and will provide an outline of the activities to be carried out in a soft systems study. However, as it is stated above, it is too vague to be a root definition, therefore the process of thinking through in detail using the CATWOE elements will be undertaken.

Customers – victims or beneficiaries

The study has been initiated by the MD of the Floppit Corporation. The likely beneficiaries of the study are the MD and the strategic management group of the Floppit Corporation. In this case the MD will be chosen as the customer. He will be affected by the study and be the recipient of its findings.

Actors

A study can be carried out by three main groups of actors; firstly by external analysts, secondly by a mixed team of both external analysts and internal participants, or thirdly by internal participants alone. The choice would depend upon the situation. In this example an external analyst team will be chosen.

Transformation

A soft systems study may be carried out for many reasons. The most obvious is that substantive findings/actions are required. However, other reasons are possible. A study may be carried out in order to train people in the use of the methodology (skill development), as part of a management team-building exercise, or as an exercise in researching SSM. A real world project will inevitably contain elements of all of these but, remembering that a human activity system model focuses only on one part of the real circumstances, in the process of developing a model a choice must be made explicitly amongst these alternatives. This does not of course rule out the idea of creating other models relevant to the conduct of a study.

In this case the provision of substantive findings will be chosen. The transformation then becomes one of transforming an MD in need of ideas about the future direction of the Floppit Corporation into an MD provided with ideas for the future direction of the corporation which are both systemically desirable and culturally feasible.

Thus: MD in need of ideas $\Longrightarrow$ T $\Longrightarrow$ MD in possession of sound ideas. This implies that the major activities of the project will be concerned with generating sound ideas and then transferring them to the MD.

Weltanschauung
There are two underlying assumptions which are implicit in this system:
1. That SSM is an appropriate, meaningful and legitimate way of tackling this strategic problem.
2. That external analysts, using SSM, are able to tackle this problem effectively.

There are a number of points to note here.
a) We are looking for the assumptions or beliefs which are implicit in the system definition, not those that we think ought to be correct.
b) The assumptions do not have to be true. It may be useful in certain circumstances to explore the implications of systems whose W is not actually valid within the circumstances of the situation under study. A system to manufacture and sell floppits at a loss might be an interesting model to use in the study but it is unlikely that the underlying W – that making a loss is a desirable, meaningful and legitimate thing to do – would actually be held to be acceptable by the MD of the Floppit Corporation.
c) The assumptions underlying the definition should not be logically contradictory – a system to give floppits away and make a profit by so doing implies the assumptions that no income is generated from floppits and that profit (income minus expenditure) is possible. This is logically contradictory. Even if giving away floppits did not cost anything (which is unlikely), profit would only be possible if expenditure were actually a negative amount. Logically, a negative expenditure would imply a source of income (other than floppits). In such circumstances it would be better to rethink the definition to focus upon the other source of profit.

Owner
This is the set of people, or system, which could decide that the system in question be destroyed. It can often be easier to ask the question 'who, or what provides legitimacy for the system, such that if this were removed the system would no longer be operable?' In the Floppit Corporation study being discussed

here it is the MD who has initiated the study and whose authority provides the legitimacy for the system in question. If he were to decide to remove that legitimacy then the system would be destroyed. In the real situation, ownership may rest on a set of quite complex relationships. For example the authority of the MD derives in itself from the board of directors and their authority in turn from the shareholders. Thus there may well be a number of options for the choice of ownership. In the modelling phase it is up to the analyst to choose the owner for the system concerned and it is sensible to choose the most direct owner. Thus in this case the sensible choice is the MD rather than the board of directors.

Environmental constraints

In a study situation such as this the major constraints upon the system are likely to be resources – the number of analysts available to the project, and time – no doubt the MD requires results within some reasonable (or maybe unreasonable) period of time. Other constraints that may be imposed might be limits upon the access to personnel or sensitive information. The environmental constraints represent what the system must take as given in its operation and therefore require some thought as to their selection.

Note: working through this example once again illustrates the careful consideration that has to be given to each element of the root definition and the choices that have to be made. It also shows that there are many possible root definitions potentially arising from one expression of a relevant system. The approach within SSM is to provide clear and coherent individual models whilst using a range of such models to explore the many complexities of the real situation.

To summarize the CATWOE elements for this root definition:

C – **The MD**

A – **External analysts**

T – **MD in need of ideas** $\implies$ **T** $\implies$ **MD with sound ideas**

W – **That external analysts using SSM is an acceptable and legitimate form of organization**

O – **The MD**

E – **The number of external analysts available (say three) and the time required to carry out the study (say two months).**

The root definition may now be stated in full:

An MD-owned system, operated and managed by three external (to the Floppit Corporation) analysts, to provide to the MD within two months a set of sound ideas (defined as both systemically desirable and culturally feasible) concerned with the future development of the Floppit Corporation through the use of soft systems methodology. The system carries this out by finding out about the situation, generating relevant models of human activity systems, comparing the models with the situation, identifying systemically desirable and culturally feasible changes to the situation, and transferring the results of the study to the MD in an effective manner. The system must operate within the resource and time constraints stated above.

Example 2. A progress reporting system

An analyst owned and operated system which fulfils the MD's desire to have frequent and meaningful information about the progress of the study. The system operates by organizing and delivering presentations to the MD which identify the activities in progress, activities completed, and activities yet to be undertaken, illustrates the results of the activities to date, provides estimates of the time to completion of other activities, and highlights any issues and problems with the conduct of the study which can be resolved through action on the part of the MD. The system is constrained by the presentation facilities available within the Floppit Corporation and the diary commitments of the MD.

Example 3. A system to provide a working environment which is both conducive to productivity and fulfilling to the staff involved

A Floppit Corporation-owned system, operated by all managerial staff to create a working environment conducive to both productivity and staff welfare by identifying those elements of the Floppit Corporation which inhibit productivity and/or staff welfare, formulating changes to the corporation which in principle should support productivity and welfare improvements, implementing change, monitoring the impact of the changes on productivity and welfare, and learning about the corporation through such activity in order to improve the identification and change of problem areas. The system is constrained by the need for on-going productive activity, the structure of the organization, limited time, and the imposition of the board of directors that expenditure on the development activity as a whole should not exceed 5% of the operating budget of the corporation.

Example 4. A Floppit manufacturing and selling system

A system to generate a commercially acceptable return upon investment by manufacturing and selling Floppit products. The system operates by acquiring the necessary components and assembling them into appropriate Floppit products as required by the orders taken for such products generated by sales activity, and distributing those products to the customers who have placed orders. The system employs the latest assembly technology and processes.

Exercises

1. Use the CATWOE framework to analyze examples 2, 3 and 4 and assess the strengths and weaknesses of these root definitions.

2. Rewrite improved versions of examples 2, 3 and 4. Provide a CATWOE analysis of your improved version.

3. Select three other relevant systems for the Floppit Corporation and construct root definitions and CATWOE analyses.

4. Generate relevant systems for each of the following:
   a. a hospital
   b. a school
   c. a local football team
   d. a television talkshow.

5. Generate a primary-task and an issue-based relevant system for each of the following:
   a. a local council
   b. a computer manufacturer
   c. a Test Match series in cricket, or the World Series in baseball.

5 Modelling human activity systems: generating models

- *Creating conceptual models*
- *Using the root definition*
- *Checking and assessing conceptual models*
- *The modelling process: a review*
- *Modelling in practice*
- *Modelling examples*

This chapter covers the processes involved in moving from a root definition to a conceptual model of a human activity system. The areas covered in this chapter correspond to concept 4 of soft systems methodology. See figure 5.1 below.

The aim of the chapter is to demonstrate the process of systems modelling. This process involves generating and structuring the minimum, but necessary, set of activities required of a system to be the system named in the root definition. The modelling of human activity systems differs in this way from the modelling processes involved in other approaches. In soft systems methodology the activity system derives from the root definition to the extent that it is possible to say that it is the root definition which is being modelled. It is to the root definition rather than to the situation that reference is made when trying to establish the contextual correctness of the model, but in addition reference may also be made to the notion of a formal systems model and to other areas of systems theory in order to try to establish the systemic correctness of the model.

Systems models in soft systems methodology are an expression of the ideal form of organized activity and are not descriptions of the real activities in a problem situation. Therefore the derivation of an activity model is a somewhat more abstract process than that normally encountered in the generation of descriptive models. It is for this reason that considerable attention is paid in this chapter to each aspect of the modelling process.

Once again it must be emphasized that good modelling is a skill which requires practice to attain and that at each stage you should try out the steps for yourself before moving on to the next.

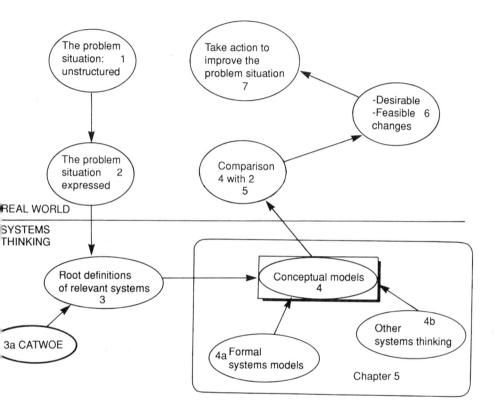

Figure 5.1 Soft systems methodology

Creating conceptual models

The idea for a system which found its first expression as a relevant system has been formalized and become a more detailed expression during the generation of a formal system name, or root definition. The next modelling process is the creation of an activity model of the system named in the root definition. This is done by assembling and structuring the minimum, but necessary, set of activities required of the system named in the root definition.

There are a number of points to note here:

1. Modelling language.

The modelling language used within soft systems methodology consists of the verbs of the English language plus arrows to indicate the relationships between the activities. The relationships are termed logical dependencies. This area will be examined in more depth later in the chapter. In soft systems methodology (SSM) the concern is with understanding purposeful human action, that is, with trying to untangle the many activities which go on, and with understanding how these activities relate to and impinge upon one another. An activity does something, and the words which express doing are verbs. Therefore the modelling language is verb-based. Often the main relationship with which modelling is concerned is that other activities must have taken place in order that an activity can proceed. For example when building a house there must be foundations before the structural framework can be erected, and the structural framework must be in place before the roof can be erected. Thus there are logical dependencies between the activities involved.

Figure 5.2 illustrates the representation of activities and logical dependencies.

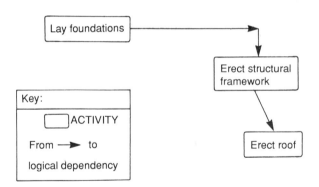

Figure 5.2   An illustration of logical dependence

Using the root definition

2. Root definition and conceptual model.

The foundation for the activity system model, or conceptual model, is the root definition. The conceptual model should contain only those activities which stem directly from the root definition together with activities necessary to ensure the coherence of logical dependency. Thus the root definition and conceptual model form a mutually supporting pair. The conceptual model should reflect only the root definition and nothing more; thus it is possible all the time to ask "Is there anything in the root definition which is not covered in the conceptual model?" and "Is there anything in the conceptual model which does not arise out of the root definition?". Mutually adjusting the root definition and conceptual model until the answer to both questions is 'No' is the core process involved in modelling. When the answer is 'No' then the condition that the conceptual model is the minimum, but necessary, set of activities to be the system named in the root definition has been met. Thus it can be argued that the model is a valid model of the system named in the root definition.

3. Capturing the elements of the root definition.
The previous discussion of the structure of root definitions defined the elements of a well-formulated root definition according to the CATWOE concept. It is to be expected therefore that the conceptual model will reflect all of these elements and that there will be activities handling these various elements.

4. The process of modelling.
   Step 1. Develop a well-formulated root definition, for example the root definition developed earlier on page 73.
An owner-owned system, manned and operated by authors which seeks to capture, organize and present the ideas, concepts and approach which form soft systems methodology in a form more appropriate to an audience than the form in which these ideas and concepts are currently encountered. The system takes as given the nature of the ideas and concepts, which are regarded as valuable both academically and practically but which are not easily available to the audience. The system must operate within the resource constraints created by the wider situation of the authors and within the technical constraints of the mode of presentation and the publisher.
   Step 2. Underline the verbs in the root definition.
An owner-owned system, <u>manned and operated</u> by authors which <u>seeks</u> to <u>capture</u>, <u>organize</u> and <u>present</u> the ideas, concepts and approach which form soft systems methodology in a form more appropriate to an audience than the form in which these ideas and concepts are currently encountered. The system <u>takes</u> as given the nature of the ideas and concepts, which are

regarded as valuable both academically and practically but which are not easily available to the audience. The system must <u>operate</u> within the resource constraints created by the wider situation of the authors and within the technical constraints of the mode of presentation and the publisher.

Step 3. Identify and extract the verbs which form the main transformation. In this case they are capture, organize, and present.

Step 4. Organize the verbs into activities and define the main logical dependencies (see figure 5.3).

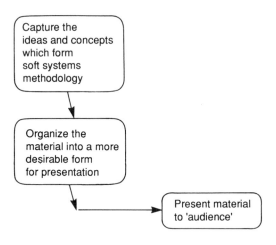

Figure 5.3   Extracting and organizing the main activities

Step 5. Consider each activity in turn and ask "What activities must go on directly prior to this activity?".

The final activity is "present material to audience". In order to carry out this activity it would be necessary to have both the material and a means of conveying that material to the audience. Given that there might also be many ways in which the material might be conveyed then it would at least be necessary to do an activity "decide how to convey material to audience".

Looking to the activity "organize material...", it would be necessary to know the desirable form before being able to carry out the activity. The results of this process are shown in figure 5.4.

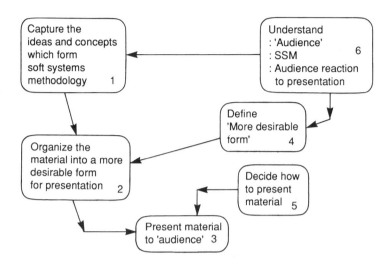

Figure 5.4 Extending the activities

The core activities of the transformation process have now been identified. If the activities were carried out as stated then the ideas and concepts forming SSM would be picked up, reorganized, and re-presented to an audience, which is precisely the transformation stated in the root definition. However the model still lacks many elements of the root definition and therefore attention must now turn to these.

Step 6. Add the control activities.

The next element to consider is the idea of system. It is fundamental to this idea that there is some form of control activity which tries to balance the demands of the different activities so that they operate together in an organized way. Such control activities will have three basic parts: 1) an activity concerned with collecting information about the system – this is referred to as monitoring; 2) an activity concerned with deciding what managerial (control) action to take; and 3) an activity concerned with taking or implementing that action. Thus the model becomes that in figure 5.5, below. This model has substantially captured the main aspects of the root definition. [You should now refer back to the root definition and compare the elements of the definition with the model.]

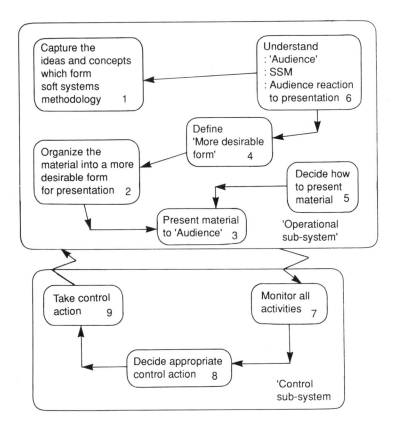

Figure 5.5 Adding the basic control activities

There are however still three elements unaccounted for, the owner, the actors, and the environmental constraints.

Step 7. Elaborate the basic model to account for other elements (figure 5.6).

Each cycle has consisted of four steps:
1. Extracting activities or elements from the root definition.
2. Identifying logical dependencies between activities.
3. Adding logical necessary activities where appropriate.
4. Checking model against root definition to see if the model is complete, or whether further development is necessary.

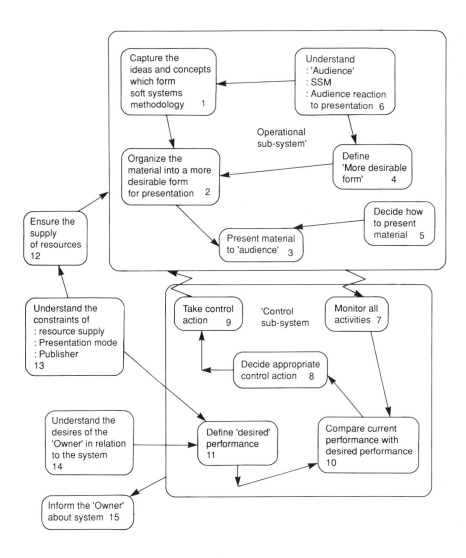

Figure 5.6 Adding the other elements – the completed model

The modelling process is complete when no further iterations are required. When this has been achieved the position should have been reached whereby all the elements of the root definition are reflected in the conceptual model. This is precisely the position needed if the model is to be a defensible representation of a human activity system. It has been emphasized on many occasions in this text that a conceptual model is not a representation of activities actually carried out in the real situation, but rather an ideal version of an organized set of activities. This creates a problem because it is not possible, therefore, to look at the situation and ask whether or not the model is correct. It is often the case with other forms of modelling that the model is really a description of some part of the real situation and therefore it is quite natural to turn to the real situation to assess the adequacy or otherwise of the model. Models of human activity systems cannot be evaluated in this way because they are not descriptive but rather are a theoretical device. In a sense they are a fantasy, a dream of what ultimately a well-organized activity system might look like if such a thing were to exist. Therefore, the problem remains of how to assess whether or not the model that has been created is acceptable as a sound model. One way of checking the model has already been mentioned – that is, comparing the model with the root definition; however, another method exists which is based upon theory and employs a concept known as the formal systems model. In the next section a checklist based upon the root definition and the formal systems model will be illustrated which provides a basis for the completeness and correctness of a conceptual model.

Checking and assessing conceptual models

A conceptual model can be validated in two ways. Firstly it can be checked against the root definition and secondly it can be checked against the generic attributes of all systems by using the formal systems model.

The idea of a system is that of an organized whole. The theory of organized wholes, or systems, has been developed in a branch of knowledge called general systems theory. This provides a general theory of systems and from this it is possible to derive a statement of the attributes of all kinds of systems. In soft systems methodology these attributes have been brought together in a framework called the formal systems model.

The formal systems model contains ten elements:

1. The system (S) has an on-going purpose or mission. This may be something which can be pursued but perhaps never achieved, or it may be more tangible and hence describable in terms of goals and objectives.

2. S has a means of assessing its performance with respect to its purpose or mission. The system must therefore be able to monitor its actual performance and assess that performance in relationship to some measures of performance.

3. S has a regulatory, or decision-making, function which can take operational action in the light of elements 1) and 2) above, to ensure an acceptable level of performance.

4. S is made up of components which are themselves systems and hence have all the attributes of a system.

5. The components of S show some degree of interaction, or connectivity. In the case of conceptual models this connectivity is based upon the idea of logical dependency. An activity is logically dependent upon another if in order to function it is necessary for that other activity to have operated to some degree before the dependent activity can operate.

6. S can be separated from the wider systems and from the environment in which it operates. The use of Customers, Owner, and Environment within CATWOE formalizes this attribute for human activity systems.

7. S is separable from its environment and wider systems, because within S the regulatory function has the power to take direct action rather than merely try to influence things. There is therefore a conceptual boundary between the system and its environment based upon the power to act.

8. S has resources which are at the disposal of the decision-making function. The human resources of the system are already covered by the notion of actor in the CATWOE framework.

9. S has some basis for continued existence and stability. The system will have some ability to recover stability if disrupted by an outside disturbance.

10. There is an observer who considers the system to be of interest. In SSM this is handled by the notion of Weltanschauung.

These ten areas can be used to frame questions about the model. Thus for example taking the model developed previously and shown in figure 5.6:

1. Purpose or mission.

   In the root definition – to communicate SSM in a better form than currently encountered.

   In the model – similar – see operational sub-system.

2. Performance.

See control sub-system, particularly activities 7, 10, 11; although the internal measure of performance is not given explicitly – this could be an area for further development of the model.

3. Regulatory function.

See control sub-system, particularly activities 8, 9.

4. Components.

There are fifteen activities and two major sub-systems, operational and control.

5. Connectivity.

Shown by the logical dependencies in the model.

6. Wider system and environment.

See activities; 1 and 6 in respect of audience and SSM, 14 and 15 in respect of the owner – the wider systems, 12 and 13 in respect of resources, modes of presentation and publishing requirements – the environmental constraints.

7. Boundary.

Not formally defined, but the regulatory function can act upon all activities within the model. There are no activities in the model outside of the power of the regulatory function.

8. Resources.

Authors are noted in the root definition and other resource constraints are mentioned in the root definition. Authors are not explicitly mentioned in the model although resource constraints are included at activities 12 and 13. Strictly the model should be amended to include authors explicitly. It might also be preferable to improve the handling of resources in the root definition and hence improve the model.

9. Coherence and continuity.

The use of a control sub-system provides some means to ensure recovery from disturbance. The model at activity 14 suggests that it is the desires of the owner of the system which would provide some momentum for continuance.

10. Observer.

This is covered by the W within the CATWOE. The inclusion of activity 4 to define a more desirable form of material, and activity 2 to organize it in that form, reflect the idea within the W that it is both possible and desirable to reorganize the presentation of material about SSM. There is nothing in the model which contradicts the underlying W.

This analysis reveals that in general the model conforms to the framework of the formal system model, but that the model does not explicitly deal with the actors element of the root definition and that the treatment of measures of performance and resources in both the root definition and model are areas in which improvements can be made.

Although nothing can guarantee a perfect model, this analysis shows that the necessary activities to be a system as defined by the given root definition have been assembled to some degree of satisfaction. The model, given some minor amendments, is therefore acceptable to be used in the comparison stage of the methodology. The process of comparison is discussed in detail in chapter 6.

The modelling process : a review

The previous sections have described the process of moving from a root definition to a conceptual model. This process has been described in terms of the steps necessary to assemble and structure the minimum, but necessary, set of activities required to be the system defined in the root definition.

The modelling process has been detailed in the form of four steps:

1. Extracting activities and elements from the root definition.
2. Identifying logical dependencies between activities.
3. Adding logically necessary activities.
4. Validating the model by use of the root definition, the CATWOE elements, and the formal system model attributes.

Further examples and exercises are provided at the end of this chapter.

Modelling in practice

At first sight, creating conceptual models seems to be a long and quite difficult process and sometimes it is argued that short cuts are preferable. Models of various sorts can be found in many textbooks so why not use those, or alternatively they can be generated without recourse to a root definition, so why bother?

The main reason is rigour. The whole aim of creating a model is to use it for analysis in the process of comparison. In this way not only does the model create an intense focus upon certain parts of a situation, allowing us to examine those parts in great detail, but also it should generate ideas for change and action. Such ideas for change and action need to be well founded. Almost anyone can just think up ideas for change, but there is no real justification for these beyond the status of the person concerned. If complex situations containing many people are to be addressed and handled in a reasonable way, then it is imperative that the analysis and arguments which lie behind any recommendations are available for scrutiny. Creating models can provide part of the documentation necessary to inform that scrutiny.

The main concern in any situation is deciding what elements of the situation are important and what elements are not. The basis of creating human activity systems models is the identification of the minimum, but necessary activities, and their relationships to one another. In this way the main elements of an area of purposeful action have been identified. These elements must be the ones to which attention is directed if a deeper understanding of the situation under scrutiny is going to be gained.

Essentially in the process of creating a model, the argument is being created which says "If some action in the real world were to be created as indicated in the name of the system (root definition) then that action would have to contain at the least the activities and relationships indicated in the conceptual model, however, they were manifested in the real situation." Thus the activities and relationships of the model provide a focus of concerns. It is upon these elements that attention should be directed and priority action based.

It should be clear by now why borrowing models or creating intuitive models is not good practice. Such models are not necessarily as rigorous in terms of being the minimum necessary elements as are those created by the modelling process described above, in other words they may lack the coherence and integrity demanded of human activity systems models. However, published models and intuitive ideas are both excellent sources of ideas for relevant systems and an informal use of such models is not to be discouraged, but before serious use of the models is made they should be examined by using the appropriate concepts involved in the modelling process to ensure that they have the highest levels of coherence and integrity. Once this has been done then the models may be used with some confidence. It is not ultimately possible to say that a model is correct in an absolute sense, but it is possible to show that the model is a rigorous representation of an activity system and hence that it is a firm foundation for the analysis which arises when the model is used in comparison.

Modelling examples

In this section further examples of creating conceptual models will be given using the root definitions concerning the Floppit Corporation generated in chapter 4.

Example 1.
   Step 1 – Develop a well-formulated root definition.
An **MD-owned system, operated and managed by three external (to the Floppit Corporation) analysts, to provide to the MD within two months a set of sound ideas (defined as both systemically desirable and culturally feasible) concerned with the future development of the Floppit Corporation through the use of soft systems methodology. The system carries this out by finding out about the situation, generating relevant models of human activity systems, comparing the models with the situation, identifying systemically desirable and culturally feasible changes to the situation, and transferring the results of the study to the MD in an effective manner. The system must operate within the resource and time constraints stated above.**

   To summarize the CATWOE elements for this root definition:
   C – The MD
   A – External analysts
   T – MD in need of ideas $\Longrightarrow$ T $\Longrightarrow$ MD with sound ideas
   **W – That external analysts using SSM is an acceptable
         and legitimate form of organization**
   O – The MD
   **E – The number of external analysts available (say three) and the
         time required to carry out the study (say two months).**

   Step 2. Underline the verbs in the root definition.
An **MD-owned system, <u>operated</u> and managed by three external (to the Floppit Corporation) analysts, <u>to provide</u> to the MD within two months a set of sound ideas (defined as both systemically desirable and culturally feasible) concerned with the future development of the Floppit Corporation through the use of soft systems methodology. The system carries this out by <u>finding out</u> about the situation, <u>generating</u> relevant models of human activity systems, <u>comparing</u> the models with the situation, <u>identifying</u> systemically desirable and culturally feasible changes to the situation, and <u>transferring</u>**

the results of the study to the MD in an effective manner. The system must
<u>operate</u> within the resource and time constraints stated above.

Step 3. Identify and extract verbs which form the main transformation.
1. <u>Finding out</u> about the situation
2. <u>Generating</u> relevant models of human activity systems
3. <u>Comparing</u> the models with the situation
4. <u>Identifying</u> systemically desirable and culturally feasible changes to the
    situation
5. <u>Transferring</u> the results of the study to the MD in an effective manner.

These activities together provide the major transformation of the system which
is given in the root definition as: <u>to provide</u> **to the MD within two months a
set of sound ideas (defined as both systemically desirable and culturally
feasible) concerned with the future development of the Floppit Corporation
through the use of soft systems methodology.**

The other major activity noted in the root definition is the control and
management activity:
6. <u>operated</u> and <u>managed</u> **by three external (to the Floppit Corporation)
    analysts,**

**Step 4. Organize the verbs into activities and define the main logical
dependencies.**

**Step 5. Consider each activity in turn and ask "What activities must go
on directly prior to this activity?"** (See figure 5.7 below.)
Notes:
1. The comparison activity may reveal inadequacies in either the knowledge
    about the situation or the model(s) that have been generated, and therefore
    there is a logical dependency between the comparison activity and the
    finding out and the generating of the model activities. For clarity these three
    activities have been grouped together (see figure 5.8 below).
2. The results of all of the first three activities feed the activity of identifying
    changes, and if the changes identified are seen as inadequate there is a
    dependency back to the first three activities. Indeed one way of viewing soft

systems methodology is as a search process to identify acceptable changes which utilizes the activities of finding out, modelling, and comparison as a means for facilitating the search.

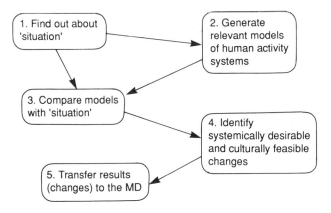

Figure 5.7   Stage 1 – modelling

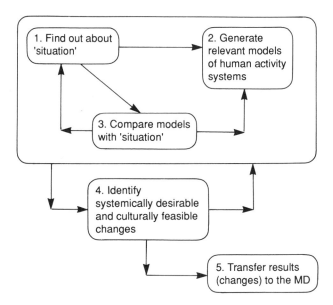

Figure 5.8   Stage 2 – modelling

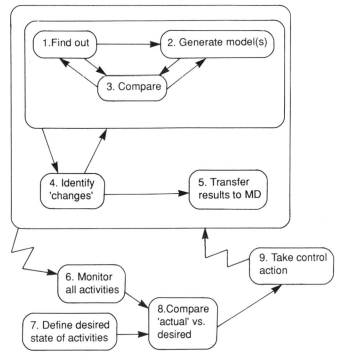

Figure 5.9   Adding the control activities

Step 6. Add the control activities. (See figure 5.9 above.)

Step 7. Elaborate the basic model to account for other elements.

Attention must now be turned to the other elements in the root definition which have not yet been taken into account in the activity model. Remember the root definition is: **An MD-owned system, operated and managed by three external (to the Floppit Corporation) analysts, to provide to the MD within two months a set of sound ideas (defined as both systemically desirable and culturally feasible) concerned with the future development of the Floppit Corporation through the use of soft systems methodology. The system carries this out by finding out about the situation, generating relevant models of human activity systems, comparing the models with the situation, identifying systemically desirable and culturally feasible changes to the situation, and transferring the results of the study to the MD in an effective manner. The system must operate within the resource and time constraints stated above.**

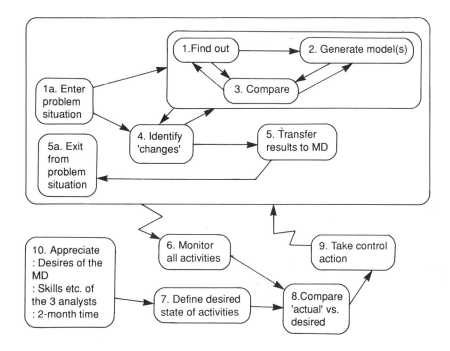

Figure 5.10 The final activity model

Considering the root definition against the activity model reveals a number of elements unaccounted for. These are:

1. **An MD-owned system**
2. **Three external (to the Floppit Corporation) analysts**
3. **Within two months**
4. **Concerned with the future development of the Floppit Corporation**
5. **The system must operate within the resource and time constraints stated above.**

Incorporation of these elements leads to a completed model. (Figure 5.10 above.)

Notes:

1. One of the major concerns was with the term external analysts. If the analyst is an external agent then there must be a process whereby the analyst first enters the problem situation in order to carry out the analysis and then leaves

the situation once the work has been completed. Including this idea in the model accounts for the incorporation of activities 1a and 5a into the model.

2. The ownership and resource elements have been amalgamated into activity 10. This is perhaps a rather coarse treatment of these elements and some expansion would be both possible and desirable, but it has been handled in this way in order to limit the number of activities in the model.

3. The notion of concern with the future development of the Floppit Corporation would be dealt with by amending the wording of some of the activities. In particular activity 5 would be reworded to say identify changes concerned with the future development of the Floppit Corporation which are both systemically desirable and culturally feasible. Format limitations have prevented this being shown in the diagram above.

Step 8. Critique of the model.

An analysis and critical appraisal of the model is carried out by using the three elements noted in section 5.4, namely:

1. the root definition
2. the CATWOE analysis, and
3. the formal systems model.

Root definition.

The process of modelling has been to extract and assemble the various elements of the root definition, thus there is a continuous checking activity operating as part of the modelling process. However it is still worthwhile to ask:

1. Is there any element of the root definition which has not been incorporated into the conceptual model?
2. Is there anything in the model which does not follow from the root definition?

In this example it is argued that the model and the root definition are compatible. It might well be argued that the use of the term 'external analyst' in the root definition is not really explicit enough as it leads to the incorporation of two major activities into the model. It could well be worthwhile to amend the root definition to make these activities a more explicit part of the definition.

The **CATWOE** for the root definition was given as:

C – **The MD**

A – **External analysts**

T – **MD in need of ideas** ⟹ T ⟹ **MD with sound ideas**

W – **That external analysts using SSM is an acceptable and legitimate form of organization**

O – **The MD**

E – **The number of external analysts available (say three) and the time required to carry out the study (say two months).**

It is evident that all these elements are embodied in the **formal systems model**.

1. Purpose or mission.

   To provide sound ideas to the MD.

2. Performance.

   Sound ideas, effectively transferred, within two months.

3. Regulatory function.

   There is a control sub-system.

4. Components.

   Model made up of activities and logical dependencies.

5. Connectivity.

   Based upon logical dependencies.

6. Wider system and environment.

   (i)   Owner.

   (ii) Time and resource constraints.

   (iii) The problem situation as external to the system.

7. Boundary.

   Not formally defined. There are no activities in the model outside of the power of the regulatory function.

8. Resources.

   The three analysts.

9. Coherence and continuity.

   Coherence given by the use of the SSM framework for enquiry as the basis for the activity model. Continuity is provided for in a limited way by the entry and exit activities and the MD's desire that the activity be undertaken.

These analyses together support the model and the rigour of the development process used.

Exercises

1. Produce models for the root definitions given in chapter four.

2. Model the following relevant systems:
   - A tea-making system
   - A conceptual model modelling system
   - A system to play chess

3. Provide one of your models to one or more colleagues who are learning about soft systems methodology and ask them to assess the model.

4. Develop models relevant to a professional football team.

5. Develop models relevant to your business or learning activities.

6. Identify a problem within your work situation, or to do with a hobby you are involved in:
   a) Produce a rich picture of the problem situation.
   b) Identify two problem areas within the problem situation.
   c) For each problem area generate two relevant systems.
   d) Generate models for each relevant system.

6 Comparison

- *The comparison process: an overview*
- *The nature of the comparison process*
- *A framework for the comparison process*
- *The methods and techniques of comparison*
- *Other techniques*
- *The comparison process revisited*
- *Beyond comparison*
- *Review*

All the hard work involved in choosing, naming and modelling human activity systems is just the foundation for the most important part of the methodology – the comparison. The modelling process has produced an ideal concept of the activities involved in carrying out some organized action which is thought to be relevant to the problem situation. The model provides a framework for taking a detailed look at the situation and for asking to what extent there are similarities and differences between the model and the situation. Assessing and evaluating these similarities and differences may suggest potential areas for change in the situation. On the other hand a comparison might suggest that a different perspective on the situation is required and hence point towards directions in which new relevant systems should be sought before starting the modelling cycle once again.

This chapter looks in detail at concept five of the methodology – comparison, as shown in figure 6.1. The modelling activities have taken place in the systems world; below the horizontal line in the diagram. The modelling has depended entirely upon logic and has not considered what is happening in the situation at all. The output of the modelling process is an expression of the minimum, but necessary, set of systemically organized activities required for the action specified in the root definition, and hence seen as potentially relevant to tackling the problems encountered in the problem situation. The time has now come to use that model in relation to the situation, and hence move toward taking some problem-solving action. It is the comparison process which helps to stimulate, facilitate and organize the thinking behind such action. This chapter will discuss the various ways in which the comparison process can be carried out and describe the methods which can be used to aid the process.

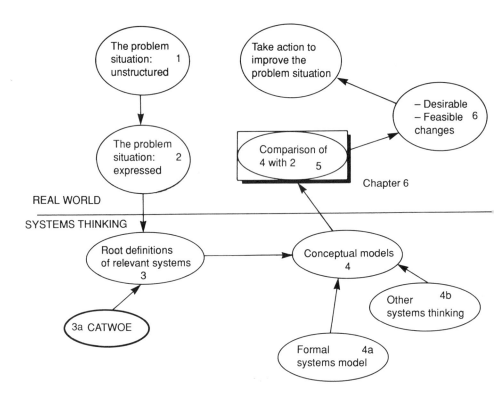

Figure 6.1   Soft systems methodology

The comparison process: an overview

The comparison process is the most important process in soft systems methodology. All of the effort involved in creating a model is to establish a firm basis for the comparison.

Comparison is a familiar process which is often taken for granted. If we wish to measure something we take a measuring stick and compare it against the item we wish to measure. The measuring stick can be standardized and thus we may measure many objects which are not physically in the same vicinity and be able to compare the objects in terms of size. Often, however, the use of comparison is more subtle, as when the judge at a dog show tries to assess each dog presented to her in relation to the image of the ideal dog which she has in her mind. She looks for the way in which the dog matches with the image and the ways in which the dog varies from the image and in this way reaches her judgement on the dogs. It is precisely this type of process that is being explicitly managed in SSM.

The core idea arising from the work on tackling ill-structured problems is that the problem-solving in this area depends upon learning the way to a solution. This process of learning depends upon juxtaposing familiar images against the real circumstances. This comparison of image with reality may make us realize that there are inadequacies in the way in which the situation is organized or indeed it may make us realize that our image is inadequate as a basis for understanding the situation. It is out of the tension of the comparison that learning can be created. The whole methodology has provided a mechanism for organizing and managing this learning process. However, it must be recognized that this learning process operates naturally, a process often labelled intuition. The role of the methodology is to provide an explicit framework through which this process can be aided and improved.

The effort involved in selecting and generating systems models is of itself valueless, it is only when the model is used in comparison that all the effort becomes worthwhile. In the modelling process every element of the model has been argued about and justified as operationally and systemically necessary, and the model may be communicated to others and evaluated by them. Thus the modelling process has been concerned with creating a clean, defensible, substantiated and communicable image. The value of producing good models is that their use in the comparison process should provide similar improvements in the defensibility, substantiation, and communicability of the learning arising out of the process. However, it is not only the model which creates improvements, but also the way in which the models are used. It is these ways of using models which is the subject of this chapter.

The nature of the comparison process

The development of soft systems methodology, and the on-going research which surrounds it, can be seen as the establishment and enhancement of ways to facilitate the learning process which forms the core of problem-solving activity. There is still a great deal to be understood about this area and the methods and techniques described throughout the rest of this chapter summarize the limits of knowledge to date. These methods and techniques provide a tried and tested set of approaches, but they do not necessarily exhaust the possibilities. The comparison process is both sophisticated and subtle, involving as it does learning in two different domains simultaneously. Learning occurs about both the situation and about the model. Questions may be raised about the relevancy of the model, that is, the degree to which the model provides a framework which aids the resolution of the problem. There is also the question about the formulation of the model, that is, the way in which the assumptions underlying the model have been handled. Finally, there is the question about the structure of the model, that is, the way in which the activities have been bounded and related together. At the same time questions may be raised about the situation, about the way in which activities are carried out, resourced, and controlled. These questions may highlight areas of weakness within the situation and hence suggest changes in the situation which are systemically desirable with respect to the model.

The example cited previously of measuring using a measuring stick takes as given both the intellectual framework of measurement employed and the appropriateness of the technology (the stick). However, consider the simple situation of trying to measure the circumference of a circle. It is obvious that we would need circular measuring sticks or the technology would have to alter. More subtly, the intellectual framework of measurement would have to change. The measuring stick approach assumes that there are two points whose distance apart is required, but in the case of the circle we do not have two points, the circumference is the locus of one point moving at a constant distance from a fixed point. In this case the circumference is measured by adding the distance between adjacent points on the circle, that is, breaking the circle into a series of straight lines, and when we take the number of points to be infinite then the sum of the distances is equal to the circumference. In this way we can approximate the circumference but never measure it directly because we cannot measure an infinitely small distance. We can of course work out other relationships involved and calculate the distance. The essence, however, is that in attempting to use our framework of measurement a situation has been found that has forced us to rethink the framework and how to use it, and hence we have learnt something by so doing.

In tackling real world problems it is much more likely that the frameworks we employ, the systems models, may need revision in the light of being used. This discussion leads to the presentation of figure 6.2, which represents the relationships involved in the comparison process as used within soft systems methodology. The situation (which includes the analysts and their backgrounds) is the source of the images which are regarded as relevant to the situation. The images are formalized according to the precepts of the modelling process by defining root definitions and then modelling these into the form of human activity system models. It may now be clearer as to why these are termed conceptual models in that they represent a formalized expression of an image; they are conceptual, rather than a would-be attempt to describe the actuality of the situation. The models are compared with the situation which creates learning about both the models and the situation. This learning may in turn lead to iteration of the modelling process and/or recognition and formulation of action to be taken within the situation itself.

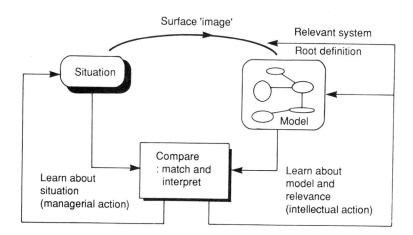

Figure 6.2 The concept of comparison

The comparison process is the core of soft systems methodology and in using the methodology the handling of the comparison is of great importance. Two ideas must be borne in mind, firstly that until the process is carried out there is no way of knowing the results it will produce (at least at any level of detail), and secondly that the process is crucial to the problem-solving effort and therefore must not be treated lightly or its impact may be lost. Three questions must therefore be addressed in planning a comparison;

1. Why is it being carried out?
2. Who should be involved?
3. What methods and techniques should be utilized?

The rest of this chapter is directed towards providing a framework for answering these questions.

A framework for the comparison process

Problem-solving projects are often quite complex activities addressing different issues as the project unfolds, iterating between stages of the methodology and involving different participants at different stages of activity. Given also the uncertainty and complexity surrounding any real world problem situation, it is not possible to provide a step-by-step approach to the conduct of a comparison in the same way as was done with the formulation of root definitions and the creation of conceptual models. Rather, a framework of considerations is presented to aid both the planning of comparisons and the understanding and interpretation of the results produced.

There are two activities involved in the comparison process: the matching of the model against the situation and the interpretation of the results produced by that matching process. The interpretation of the results depends upon two factors, firstly the degree of confidence (or of relevancy) associated with the model, and secondly the primary aspect of the situation being addressed; whether the focus is upon operational aspects of the situation, improving communication between participants in the problem-solving episode, or exploring the assumptions underlying different perspectives on the situation. These last three types are termed analytical, dialogical, and ideological respectively.

There are three modes of using a model within the comparison process depending upon the degree of confidence in the model which is held. The first is exploratory. This is the lowest degree of confidence, and therefore any model can be treated as of this type. In the exploratory mode the comparison is conducted as a basis for assessing the relevancy of the model. The comparison process will also generate a deeper understanding of, and knowledge about, aspects of the problem situation. The interpretation of the matching process is therefore concerned with both the model and the situation, but is treated as general and to be confirmed by other analysis. This is the most general form of the comparison process and all new models are subjected to it as they are used for the first time.

Once some degree of relevancy has been established the model may be used in diagnostic mode. In this mode the strengths and weaknesses of the situation as a reflection of the activity system being used are assessed and the areas of weakness identified provide a focus of attention and a basis for suggesting changes.

In the final mode, that of design, the model is used as the basis for suggesting detailed courses of action for bringing about change in the situation and for formulating an agenda for action. The relationship of these three modes of interpretation is illustrated in figure 6.3.

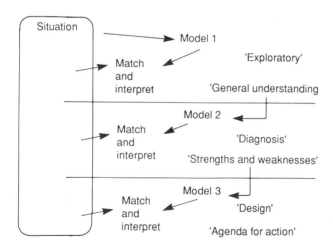

Figure 6.3 Exploratory, diagnosis and design modes of comparison

Note: Models 1, 2 and 3 may be the same model, or they may be different models generated as a result of iteration through the process.

A second dimension has already been noted in the form of the type of investigation being pursued, i.e. whether it is analytical, dialogical, or ideological.

An analytical investigation is focused upon the operations and activities within the problem situation, whereas both dialogical and ideological investigations are concerned with exploring the perspectives held by various groups of actors in the situation. A dialogical comparison is used to seek better communication between participants and would involve the comparison of one view of the situation (as expressed in a model) with a slightly differing view (or model). In this way the similarities and differences between the models can be explored as an aid to overcoming communication, or other, difficulties that participants are experiencing. For example it might be used to explore the differences between a market-oriented view of a company (probably held by the marketing department) and a production-oriented view (as held by the production department) and as an aid to formulating a jointly held view within which each perspective plays a part.

An ideological analysis would press further and explore the differences of perspective at the level of Weltanschauung (or the taken-for-granted values and assumptions which form the core of a perspective). For example, the activities which constitute a university may be perceived from at least three perspectives; as a process of knowledge creation, as a process of teaching, and as a process of administrating and managing a large operational institution. Experience suggests that many universities experience tensions, and even conflicts, which stem from the different values and taken-for-granted assumptions which underlie these three perspectives. One of the major aspects of management within a university is balancing the often conflicting demands of these three perspectives. Surfacing and formalizing the values and assumptions underlying these distinct perspectives may help to provide support for the difficult balancing act that is required in these circumstances.

The methods and techniques of comparison

At this point however it is time to look in some depth at the four main techniques for carrying out comparison, that have been developed and used extensively, these are:

1.   Structured data collection and tabulation
2.   Model to model
3.   Model overlay
4.   Attribute mapping

Each approach will be described and illustrated in turn.

Structured data collection

Structured data collection, or "structured questioning" as it is sometimes referred to, is the most basic method of carrying out a comparison. It may be carried out with any type of relevant system and any mode of use. It is particularly useful at the exploratory stage but may also be used to advantage in diagnosis. Textbook examples often combine the requirements of the exploratory and diagnosis modes, but this may lead to difficulty in interpreting the results of the comparison. It is for this reason that these modes will be treated separately here.

The main aim of the exploratory stage of comparison is to assess the relevancy of the model in the context of the problems being investigated. The basic question to be addressed is to what extent the activities in the model are actually carried out in the situation under investigation. In other words to investigate the match between the model and the situation. The basic question to be asked is thus "Does this activity exist or not?".

It is not however necessarily a straightforward matter to assess the existence or not of an activity. Firstly, real world activity is often very complex and secondly activity may be carried out very formally and intentionally, or very informally and unintentionally. It is the aim of using the model to provide a framework for helping to make sense of the real situation; therefore attempting to establish the degree of relationship between the model and the situation must be considered very carefully. To this end the approach is to generate a set of questions based on each activity in the model, the answers to which will establish the existence or otherwise of that activity. (See figure 6.4 below.)

The problem is made somewhat more difficult because of the differing nature of the things being compared. The model represents an ideal of what activities are necessary to be the system. The real world however is different in that it is only one manifestation of how an activity may be performed, the relationship being that in principle there may be many different ways of carrying out the same activity; in other words there may be many 'hows' for a particular 'what'. Therefore the question being addressed is whether there is a particular 'how', a set of actions, in the situation which corresponds to a particular 'what' in the system model.

The answer to the problem is to consider some basic systems theory. Each activity in the model can itself be thought of as a system and thus in the most basic form of a system considered to be an input, transformation, output mechanism. Whilst the existence of a particular input does not imply the existence of the system, the existence of the output does so. Therefore, if something in the real situation corresponds to the output that would be generated by a particular activity, then this would indicate the existence of a means for producing the output (a how) and hence the existence of a match between the model activity and the real world action. The question can thus be restated in the form "Is there evidence that a thing exists in the real situation which corresponds to the output of an activity in the model, and is there evidence of a mechanism (how) that produces that thing?". Indeed in most cases if the 'thing' only exists through the action of a human agent then its very existence can be taken as necessitating the existence of the how that produced it, and this is generally the case in human activity systems.

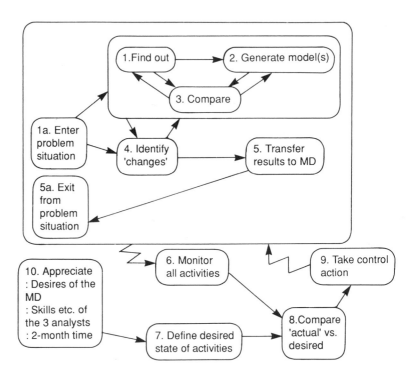

Figure 6.4   The final activity model

COMPARISON TABLE

Activity No.	Required Output	Situation	Present "How"	Exist Y/N	Comment
1a.	Analysts in situation	Project was undertaken	Invite by MD	Y	
1.	An initial understanding	Rich Pictures Issue List	By analysts	Y	From project documentation
2.	Conceptual models	Produced	By analysts	Y	-"-
3.	Matchings and interpretations	Produced	By analysts	Y	-"-
4.	Identified changes	Results	By analysts	Y	Report
5.	Analysts out of situation	Project completed	Agreement with MD	Y	
6.	Data about activities	Activity reports	By analysts	Y	Project documentation
7.	Expected state	Project plan	By analysts	Y	-"-
8.	Matching of expected versus actual	Project control meetings	By analysts	Y	-"-
9.	Control action	Reallocation of resources	By analysts	Y	-"-
10.	Understanding: Desires of MD,	Project remit	Analysts and MD	Y	-"-
	Skills etc.,	Project plan	Analysts	Y	-"-
	Time constraint	Project plan	Analysts		-"-

It is now possible to define the steps involved in an exploratory comparison based upon structured data collection. The steps are:

1. List all activities in the model.
2. Define the outputs from each activity.
3. Investigate the situation and obtain evidence that something exists which matches the output (or not).
4. Interpret and evaluate the results produced by the matching process.

An exploratory comparison using structured data collection

This example uses the example conceptual model generated in chapter 5. The comparison is set out in tabular form above. This tabulation is the result of carrying out the first three steps of the comparison, but does not include the interpretation stage.

Notes:

This table has matched each activity in the model against elements in the situation by carrying out 3 steps in the matching process:

1. List all activities
2. Define necessary outputs
3. Identify matching elements in the situation.

The fourth step in the process is to interpret the findings from the matching process. This interpretation depends upon whether a good or a bad match is expected between the model and the situation, which in turn depends upon the reasons for choosing the relevant system upon which the model is based in the first place. For the purposes of this example consider the following scenario. A project has been carried out by three analysts on behalf of the MD. They were to conduct the project using soft systems methodology. The MD, being a cautious person, has requested an evaluation of the project before implementing any of the recommendations proposed by it.

The choice of the relevant system used above was made in order to ascertain whether SSM was actually used in the project, and if so the strengths and weaknesses of the mode of use adopted by the analysts concerned. It is therefore expected that there will be a good match between the activities in the model and the actions carried out in the project.

There are actually 3 possible ways in which the model and the situation could match. There could be a good match, a poor match, or a weak match depending upon how many of the activities in the model can be seen to exist in the situation. In the situation in which the activities of the model are expected to be present in the situation a good match would arise where there was evidence that all activities were indeed carried out. A poor match would be where the evidence suggested that none of the activities were carried out, and a weak match would be where the evidence showed that only some of the activities were carried out. The weak area can be sub-divided further based upon the operational, control, and other activities which are present in a model. Only if operational activities are present, which actually create the kind of output from the system that the model requires, can the comparison truly be said to be weak. It is a very unlikely situation indeed in which the necessary control activities would be present without any operational activities. It is more usually the case that there is a good match with the operational activities but that some of the control activities are unmatched.

In the expected case a good match would indicate the need to look in more detail at the situation. A weak match would indicate structural problems and hence areas in which real activities might be implemented. A poor match is a major surprise which would, at the very least, suggest the need to choose other relevant systems but would also suggest that some fundamental rethinking of the situation is in order.

The following is a general guide to the interpretation step:

1. Good match. The conceptual model provides a good framework for making sense of the situation.

   Action:

   a) Increase the resolution level of model, by defining root definitions and models for each of the activities in the original model. Carry through the comparison at the new level, and/or

   b) increase the resolution of the comparison to the diagnostic level.

2. Weak match. This is more difficult to define because it tends to depend upon the degree of weakness and how well the model makes sense of the situation.

   a) Move to the diagnostic level and consider the implications of the missing activities on the overall system operation.

b) Make minor amendments to the root definition and remodel to see if there is any gain in match.

c) Select new relevant systems based upon any directions indicated by the new understanding of the situation that has been created by the comparison.

3. Poor match. This is the situation of greatest surprise because it challenges the implicit expectations about the situation which guided the choice of relevant system in the first place. It represents the greatest challenge, but also creates the greatest learning opportunity. It suggests that there is a need for a fundamental rethink of ideas about the situation and hence the formulation of what appear to be radical relevant systems.

Note that in the situation in which a match is unexpected, then the good match and the poor match situations are reversed.

In this section an exploratory comparison has been demonstrated. It consists of 4 steps:

1. List all activities
2. Define necessary outputs
3. Identify matching elements in the situation
4. Interpret the resulting match as good, weak or poor and either proceed to next stage of comparison or iterate back to the selection of relevant systems.

Diagnosis and Design

The exploratory stage has been concerned with assessing the relationship between the model and the situation. Once it has been established that a model bears some reasonable relationship to the area of the situation under review then consideration can move to a more detailed look at the situation and its problems. The detailed review of the situation, which is aimed at trying to understand how problems have arisen within it, is termed diagnosis. The later definition of changes within the situation, aimed at alleviating the problems, is termed design.

The basis of diagnosis is to ask questions concerning how the activity of interest is actually carried out in the situation. The range of questions will depend upon the context, but as a general guide the following would be a good starting point, therefore the following questions should be asked of every activity in the model;

a)   Who carries out the activity?

b)   What resources such as materials, money, technology and skills, are utilized in carrying out the activity?

c) How is the activity planned and controlled, and by whom?
d) What information is received to help plan and operate the activity, and what information has to be produced for others?
e) How does the activity gain its necessary inputs, and from where?
f) How does the activity get its output to the recipients of the output?

It is unlikely that such detailed information will have been collected during the first investigation of the situation; therefore it is likely that a second round of investigation will be required. The amount of effort required to obtain and assemble all of this information should not be underestimated. A great deal of time can be spent on this stage; therefore it is sound practice to think very carefully about what aspects of the situation are important in the particular context in which you are working and to develop a plan for the collection, assembly, and interpretation of the information. As the investigation progresses you may well notice new issues in the situation and recognize potential areas for improvement and you should of course record these issues and potential changes for later use. Good organization is essential at this stage; in large investigations the use of database technology can be invaluable. Consider this, most models have about 10 activities within them; therefore expanding each activity to the next level of resolution will give 10 x 10 = 100 activities, which would of course provide a fairly thorough analysis of an organization; further answering all of the questions given above will easily generate 10 statements about each activity and thus you are going to be dealing with over 1000 items of information. Clearly good planning and organization is essential.

This form of analysis is very much concerned with the operational capability of the organized actions carried out in the situation. Therefore, evaluation of the situation can be based upon performance criteria. Three such criteria would be efficacy, efficiency, and effectiveness. Efficacy is actually producing the desired output, efficiency is the ratio of the output produced divided by the resources required to produce the output, and effectiveness is a measure of how good this way of doing things is in relation to the other activities that must be carried out overall. Efficacy has been used by us previously, although not by that name. At the exploratory stage the presence or absence of the desired output from an activity was used as the basis of the comparison. Thus the comparison assessed, perhaps crudely, the efficacy of actions in the situation as a manifestation of the activities in the systems model. At this stage however the situation is being considered in more detail.

The basic form of the approach is to define measures of efficacy, efficiency, and effectiveness for each activity in the model, and to assess both the current actual performance and the desired performance.

Consider activity 5 in the model given above, namely "Transfer results of the analysis to the MD", where it would be possible to evaluate that activity in the following way.

1. Efficacy.

The output of the activity is the formal transfer of the results of the study to the MD. This has been done in the situation by the analysts using the mechanism of a report. The project generated many results; therefore the efficacy of this activity might be measured in terms of the number of results transferred to the MD (in absolute terms), or as the ratio or percentage of results produced by the study that were actually transferred. For example, if the study generated 30 potential changes to the situation but the report contained only the 15 changes considered most important by the analysts, then the actual performance achieved would be measured as 50%.

2. Efficiency.

Let us assume that it took 10 person-days of effort to produce the report then the actual performance could be assessed in terms of output (15 results) divided by resources (10 person-days) giving a measure of 1.5 results per person-day.

3. Effectiveness.

The question being addressed here is whether the approach used to transfer the results was adequate or inadequate. The activity would be effective if the MD confidently understood the results that had been transferred. This does make us consider in more depth what the activity is about. The MD has the report and therefore has possession of the results, but is this all that is required? In the scenario set up for this exercise the MD has asked for a review of the study and this would indicate some lack of confidence in, or understanding of, the results that had been provided by the study. Thus it might be concluded that the activity had been ineffective in some way. This analysis might be carried out more formally by asking the MD to rate each result in terms of (say) understanding, confidence etc. and thereby formally determining some measurement of the effectiveness of the activity.

It must be borne in mind, when assessing the results of this type of analysis, that we are interested in the overall system, and thus measures of efficacy, efficiency, and effectiveness should be created at the system level as well as at the individual activity level. There may often have to be trade-offs between one activity and the next in order to achieve the desired overall system performance. In the example discussed above it does not really matter how well the rest of the system operated if the activity of transferring the results is inadequate. It might well be better to devote more resources to this latter activity to improve system performance overall, even though this might degrade the performance at the level of some of the other activities.

The diagnosis process highlights the strengths and weaknesses of the various activities involved in the situation. It should also highlight areas in which change is desirable and suggest potential changes. Defining measures of performance also provides a framework for assessing the impact of proposed changes, and the results of implemented changes. The design process looks at these changes in more detail.

The design process must consider two problems. The first is the agenda of changes which are considered desirable and the second is the mechanism for creating those changes. Organized purposeful action in the real world is not like a motor-car or an aeroplane in which new components may simply be designed and put into operation, but is rather a creation of people acting together. Therefore people have to change the way in which they act in order to improve things. Simply pointing out that improving the effectiveness of some action is desirable, or that a change in the form of the action is required will not necessarily bring those changes about. This is one of the main reasons for trying to involve people in the problem-solving process. If they understand the reasons for the changes, have some ownership of them and commitment towards them, then they are more likely to change their way of doing things, thereby making the changes a natural outcome of using the methodology.

A more formal and detailed way of tackling the change issue is of course to regard it as the current problem to be solved and to create a model of the activities involved in bringing about such change. This will in turn allow a consideration of how each activity may be carried out, which in turn provides a plan, or agenda of actions, to be carried out. This is another cycle of the modelling process which has already been dealt with in some detail in this book.

In summary therefore this approach to comparison involves the following:

1. Exploratory comparison.

   Assessing the match between model and situation

   Output – good, weak, or poor.

2. Detailed comparison (or diagnosis); if the match is good.

   Assessing how activities are carried out and their performance on the dimensions of efficacy, efficiency, and effectiveness.

   Output – agenda of changes.

3. Design phase.

   A new methodological cycle taking the creation of the changes as the problem. Development of appropriate models.

   Output – agenda of actions, action plan, action to change.

Other techniques

The other techniques available, namely model-to-model, model overlay and attribute mapping, are techniques somewhat more specialized than those of structured data collection.

Model-to-model

In some circumstances we may be concerned with looking at one conceptual model versus another. This can be particularly useful when there are two or more different versions of what might be going on in the situation and which are fairly similar. Thus assessing the similarities and differences may lead to a deeper understanding of aspects of looking at the situation.

For example, suppose that a particular department of an organization is being considered. The department may only carry out some of the activities associated with a particular system of activity or it may carry out activities which are common to a number of systems of activity. It may be useful to describe the department in terms of the activities that it carries out. This is not conceptual modelling as previously discussed, but rather a simple description of the department in activity terms. In such a case there would be no attempt to make the model systemically coherent (by using the SSM modelling techniques). The activities in the model of the department would then be compared with activities in systems models created in the normal way. This is illustrated in figure 6.5. Once again the basic technique is that of matching, as was used in exploratory comparison. Figure 6.5 also illustrates the basic idea of the model overlay technique.

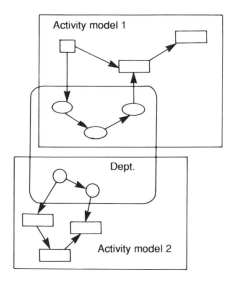

Figure 6.5 Comparing models

Model overlay and attribute mapping

One of the major problems of the standard data collection and tabulation form of comparison is the sheer amount of information that can be generated and has to be handled. There is often a need to consider or highlight one dimension of the information, and it is in these circumstances that model overlay and attribute mapping techniques have proven useful.

The activity system models developed in SSM describe the minimum, but necessary, set of activities required as the basis for some organized action. In addition the activities are structured according to their logical dependence, or interaction, with each other. In the real situation, however, there may be other forms of dependency to be considered. The structure of an organization will in part be a product of the history of the organization, the people who make up the organization, and considerations of managerial responsibility etc. It can often be very useful to consider how the actual organizational structure interacts with the basic activities which the organization, or a part of the organization, embodies. In such a case it can be useful to overlay the organizational boundaries on the activity model. An example of this is given in figure 6.6.

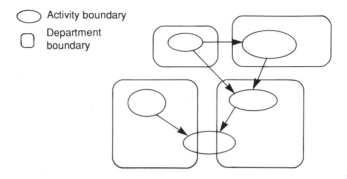

Figure 6.6   Illustration of model overlay

The simple set of five activities in the model is shown to be carried out by four different departments. Firstly, there are a number of areas where it is suggested that the output from one activity, plus any information concerning it, must be transferred to another department within the organization. Secondly, it would appear that the final activity is carried out jointly by two departments. Thus to operate the activities as required, the cooperation of different departments is necessary, but often this can be difficult. Each department may have a different view of what it is doing or a different set of priorities for the activity etc. The model overlay technique is a useful way of exploring these relationship and boundary problems.

A slightly different but related technique is that of attribute mapping. In this technique the particular attribute of interest is mapped onto the activity model. Consider for example the situation in which an information system, such as a database, has been provided to support the operation of a particular part of an organization. An activity model has been developed of that part of the organization and we are concerned with analyzing the use of the information system. An activity may be an information provider, an information user, or both. These attributes may be mapped onto the activity model. An example is shown in figure 6.7. Each activity is coded as P = Provider, or U = User.

Three activities provide input to the database and three activities use the output from the database. However one activity does not use the information system at all. Although it could possibly be a genuine situation that the one activity did not need any information or indeed do anything which created new information, this is unlikely (only further investigation in a real situation could determine the case). It would seem more likely that either potentially valuable data was going unrecorded, or that information from other sources was being employed in the activity. In either case it would suggest that there were deficiencies in the design of the information system concerned. For example, the activity might be carried out by a department that did not have access to the information system. Such an analysis might be fundamental to the definition of the basis of a specification for a new information system.

The basic approach of both model overlay and attribute mapping is to use the activity system model as a coherent framework for structuring the often complex and confusing information about the real situation in a simple and easily understood way, such that the areas of interest can be scrutinized in an organized way.

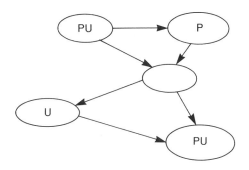

Figure 6.7   Illustration of attribute mapping

The comparison process revisited

The comparison process lies at the core of soft systems methodology (SSM). The basis of the process is straightforward; it is the comparison, or juxtaposition, of a rigorously derived coherent human activity system model against the situation. The point however is that the situation is not unproblematic. In the first stages of SSM an understanding of the real world circumstances was developed and it is this understanding that forms the situation. There may indeed be many versions of the situation, depending upon who is involved in the problem-solving activity. The process of modelling and comparison sets up challenges to that understanding. Maybe a model which was thought to be relevant turns out not to be so, or through the comparison areas are identified which were unrecognized in the original understanding. Thus a learning process is undertaken in which the 'situation' is challenged and changed until, hopefully, a better understanding, or version of the situation, is created such that responsible meaningful action can be taken to resolve the problems that created the process in the first place. However, such actions create new situations and new problem-solving activity. What is being addressed is the on-going, never-ending process of management.

It is because the nature of the process is learning, that the comparison stage is both difficult to describe or prescribe. The range of tools and techniques available support the rigour of the process. Yet often, particularly when working with the involved actors in the problem situation, it is the simple and unexpected result that has the most impact.

The concern may centre upon improvement to the on-going actions in the problem situation. In this case the choice of primary-task models and the use of the detailed comparison techniques given above is recommended. At the other extreme the concerns may be strategic and must be approached through exploration of the various issues which emerge. In this circumstance the choice of issue-based models, with perhaps little more than an exploratory comparison, is in order. The issues may arise from different versions of the situation, in which case creating a debate and a comparison of the different versions as expressed in different models is in order. This is dialogical comparison. Most fundamental of all are concerns which severely challenge the orthodoxy of the situation and require coming to grips with the core assumptions of the understanding of the situation. This is the ideological comparison approach.

Another point to note is that the learning arising from the comparison process may be of two types; learning about the situation, and learning about the models (and hence the thinking being employed in the process). As the learning about the situation unfolds and develops it will, hopefully, lead to the formulation of managerial action. On the other hand learning about the models may lead back to previous stages of the methodology, to the collection of new information, the recognition of new issues, the formulation and modelling of new relevant systems and hence to the conduct of new comparisons. Thus it can clearly be understood that the process of the methodology is cyclic and iterative in nature.

There is yet another level of learning which arises and that is learning about the practice of SSM. Each new context encountered, each new model created and compared, creates new understanding about how to use the concepts that form SSM, perhaps suggests new techniques and approaches, or simply challenges the understanding of the approach. It is in this way that fresh knowledge is gained about both SSM and the processes of management which it supports.

There is still much to be learned about the process of comparison and the practice of supporting the processes of management. This chapter has provided an introduction to the basic processes and techniques involved. These form a sound and rigorous foundation for practice, but there are still a lot of surprises to be found.

Beyond comparison

Comparison is designated as concept 5 of the methodology and beyond it are the identification of systemically desirable and culturally feasible changes (concept 6), and action aimed at changing the situation (concept 7). To some extent these areas have been addressed already through the use of the design mode of comparison. Further the separation of concept 5 – the comparison, from concept 6 – the debate about acceptable change, is at the level of logical necessity rather than at the level of practice. Technically, the comparison process identifies changes which are systemically desirable in that they arise from the application and use of human activity system models. However, in any problem situation the formal analysis will only address a limited set of the issues which form the situation. To be effective any change must have the support, understanding and commitment of those who must change, and thus the changes must be culturally feasible.

Consider the case study given in chapter 2. A good match was found between the situation and an undesirable model, and thus it was quite easy to identify systemically desirable changes to alleviate the problem situation. The most obvious would be to employ the Army officers concerned in an IT specialist position immediately they were qualified, hence improving their specialist skills, tapping their enthusiasm, and maintaining their commitment to the organization. However, such a suggestion goes directly against the established way of doing things and the cultural attitude of generalism rather than specialism. Here is an example of a systemically desirable change which is not also culturally feasible. It would of course be possible to achieve this, given wholesale changes to the military culture but it must be considered that achieving such change in relation to an issue, relatively unimportant to a particular context, is highly unlikely. In the circumstances it seemed more likely that changes aimed at improving the perceived status of the IT specialist within the culture would be both more acceptable and more efficacious.

This is not to suggest that culture is immutable or that changes can be readily designed to be acceptable, but rather that any change in a human community will have cultural dimensions. Change must be assimilated by the culture. If assimilated positively the change will be supported, whereas if assimilated negatively the change may be resisted. It is for this reason that the debate stage is made a separate concept within the methodology. To be effective the action to change (concept 7) must be understood, negotiated, and assimilated by the people whose action, or changed patterns of behaviour, will bring about the desired changes to the problem situation.

In practice a number of strategies have been adopted to take account of the culturally feasible aspects of a study. At one end of the spectrum, SSM may be operated in a totally participative mode. In this way the people concerned with the problem act as the problem-solving system and operate the methodology themselves. However, this can itself lead to the type of trap discussed in chapter 3 in which, perhaps inadvertently, the methodology is utilized to support the current thinking in the situation rather than being used to evaluate and challenge that thinking. In these circumstances an SSM specialist might be used to provide methodological guidance only. However, there are often good reasons for bringing in an outside consultant to carry out some of the substantive elements of a study. Outsiders are just that, they do not have the taken-for-granted understanding of the culture and therefore may question things in ways that insiders do not. Further, they are more likely to be outside of the internal politics and can therefore break the rules in ways that insiders cannot, and therefore they can question and examine in a way that insiders might be reluctant to. There may of course also be purely practical reasons for using outsiders. The organization may not have the resources to spare, methodological skills, or domain expertise (such as IT knowledge) that may be required to tackle a particular problem situation, and in these cases the use of specialist outsiders is seen as desirable.

The problem therefore for any outside analyst is how to engage the people in the situation in the debate about change. Put simply, the problem is how to transfer effectively the insights gained from the formal analysis carried out within

SSM to the concerned actors in the problem situation; effective being defined as the degree of assimilation of the insights by the concerned actors. The means for achieving the transfer are written reports, verbal reports, meetings, presentations, and the involvement of people in the processes of the methodology. Simply producing a list of recommendations out of the analysis and hoping that they will be acted upon is not enough, either from a methodological perspective or from a practical perspective. The user of SSM must necessarily tackle the transfer problem directly.

It is difficult to provide general guidelines for this area as each problem context provides different challenges, but the following provides a starting point.

The concept of the human activity system, as used within systems modelling, suggests that there will be a set of roles associated with any activity system. These will be the actors concerned, the victims or beneficiaries, and the owners of the activity. Any specific change implies an activity or set of activities and hence the set of roles above. Therefore for each change developed it can be worthwhile asking:

1. Who must change their actions as a result of this change?
2. Who will receive the output of this changed action?
3. Who provides input to this changed action?
4. Who owns or is responsible for this changed action?

Answering these questions defines the coalition of roles who a) will be directly affected by the change, and b) must assimilate the change into their everyday actions. If the change is to be acceptable and operable then an accommodation must be reached by this coalition on this issue. It is this coalition with whom the debate about change must be engaged or, in other words, they are the people to whom the insights of the analysis must be transferred as they are the ones who must act differently in the future. Therefore, it is also advisable to investigate the communication patterns within this coalition and consider how the material from the investigation can be suitably introduced into this pattern of communication.

In principle this concept is appealing but in a situation in which there may be many actors, many issues, many changes, and many forms of communication, handling the transfer of insights can both be difficult to achieve effectively and consume a great deal of time. However, this area is crucial if purposeful action arising from the analysis is to take place. It can of course be extremely helpful to consider the problem of transferring ownership of the insights to the affected actors as one to be addressed in a cycle of the methodology, and hence to explore relevant systems as a basis for planning and operating the transfer process.

Review

Chapters 2, 3, 4, 5 and 6 have provided a detailed statement of the methods and techniques employed within the overall framework of soft systems methodology. In places the methods and techniques have been annotated with thoughts and suggestions for use which have arisen out of practical experience of applying the methodology. The methodology provides a flexible framework for the management of problem-solving activity and as such may enhance that activity. However, it should be remembered that the methodology cannot be made a substitute for that activity. The methodology is not an algorithm which can be followed step-by-step with the guarantee of a required result at the end of the line, but rather it is closer to a heuristic device. The methodology, as portrayed within this book, consists of seven concepts which bear logically contingent relationships to each other. In any real application of the methodology the focus of interest at any time will move from one concept to another. The pattern of a real project therefore will be a complex set of moves from one focus to another, such that the methodological framework provides a language for describing, explaining and managing the process of real world problem-solving. In this way the methodology is not a description of the real world activity, but rather a conceptual model through which we can begin to make sense of the complex of actions which make up a project. In this way a project may be managed in a purposeful manner rather than as a random process of trial and error.

The methodology provides an organized approach to navigating between four streams of continuous activity which can be thought of as constituting collective purposeful activity. These are:

1. The formulation of impressions.
   - The acquisition of observations and communications.
   - The formulation of initial impressions using concepts such as problem situation, problem-solver, problem-owner, roles-values-norms, culture etc., and utilizing methods of expression such as the concept of the rich picture.
2. The evaluation and critical appraisal of impressions.
   - The recognition of relevant frameworks related to the impressions, using the concept of relevant systems.

- The exposition of the framework as a logically coherent form, using the modelling process based on the concepts of root definitions, conceptual models, human activity system, and the theory of systems.
- The examination of the relationship between the framework and the activity apparent in the situation, using the concept of comparison.

3. The assimilation of the insights gained from evaluation and critical appraisal into the human community which forms the basis of the activity in the problem situation.

   - Using the concept of formulating the debate.

4. Action in relation to the problem situation.

It is in this way that soft systems methodology provides a framework for managing the process of becoming informed which lies at the core of purposeful (informed) activity. The methodology therefore provides a general basis for managing information as a process of sense-making, discovery, and learning.

Exercises

1. Consider your situation in reading this book. Construct a model relevant to your situation and carry out an exploratory comparison using the data collection and tabulation method.

   What did the comparison tell you about your situation?

2. Consider your study class, or a group of interested friends, and consider the problems involved in transferring your understanding of SSM to them.

   - Develop a short presentation about SSM.
   - Develop a short report about SSM.
   - Develop a simple exercise related to SSM for your group to tackle.

   i)   What did you learn from these developments?

   ii) How efficacious, efficient, and effective were your activities in transferring your knowledge?

Part III

Reflections

Previous chapters have taken the reader through the methodology. This part is not meant to be a point of closure but rather a call for reflection and iteration. Learning demands that we return to what we have first learnt and see what we can gain from revisiting the demands of the learning exercise. It would be strange to aim to close down a book at the linear end point, when an iterative and reflective view of learning is paramount to the book. Because of this, the final section takes the reader back into the book and reflects on what has been dealt with.

The first reflection is in chapter 7 where the study discussed in chapter 2 is revisited. This is now looked at from a view of asking what happened as a social learning process. That learning is about the methodology as well as about the situation. We argue that a methodology is only a starting point for action and that users need to be aware of limitations in both the methodology and in themselves. The final chapter returns to the learning process of the book in relation to the managing of information. The initial view expressed in the introductory chapter is developed further and the methodology is revisited to contextualize it in this view. This concludes the argument, but hopefully not the learning!

7 Using the methodology

- *Change*
- *Action*
- *Participation*
- *The use of the methodology*
- *Revisiting the rhetoric: the problem situation*
- *Doing a cultural analysis of the problem situation:*
    pain and discovery
- *Modelling*
- *Action, change, and exit*
- *Success or failure?*
- *Conclusions*

The preceding chapter has gone into some detail to describe the systemically desirable aspects of comparison. Looking at the seven-stage model of soft systems methodology as shown in figure 2.1, we see that the analysis of comparison cuts across stages five and six. This is the problem with the seven-stage model. It does not make separations which are always useful between the sets of activities. The revised model of the methodology as shown in figure 2.2 is of more use when considering where we are now in relation to the methodology. We have just dealt with comparison of the models with the perceived real situation and are now moving on to the phase dealing with action needed to improve the situation. Going back to the seven-stage model shows that we have not yet considered culturally feasible change. This chapter deals with considerations of change, particularly culturally feasible change, and attention is paid to action and how it may be achieved.

There is a great difference between the principles of the methodology and the application of those principles to the use of the methodology in a real situation. The earlier chapters particularly stressed this. Here, we are looking at the principles of action and change implied by the methodology and then moving on to look at the practice of change and action when using the methodology. This second perspective deals with the role of the user of the methodology and deals with questions regarding responsibility, accountability, and individual and participative capabilities amongst others. The study presented in chapter 2 will be returned to so that some of these issues can be addressed.

Change

It may seem a trite statement to make, but change is eternal. Change has fascinated philosophers for centuries. It is the basis of scientific thought as well as a central theme in many of the arts. Expressing what change is becomes an awesome task. Even more difficult is the task of dealing with questions of constancy and identity. This is not the place to enter into philosophical discussion but it is still necessary to consider what change in problem situations is.

Problem situations are constructions, that is, they are perceptions of unease. It follows, therefore, that changing problem situations demands changing perceptions. Talk of being trapped by perceptions has been fundamental to this book. The methodology provides a way to discover alternative perceptions and so see the way out of traps by making them more visible. The models are used to help clarify that perceptual process and to provide a means of structuring the debate so that the socially constructed perceptions may be unfolded. But the situation is not a fixed entity which stays constant for the period of modelling and through to comparison. Every act of enquiry which occurs in the use of the methodology feeds some construction of the situation back to those involved in that situation. This creates learning, which creates new perceptions, which creates change.

In this constant change some things appear to be less transient. The feelings of unease are often linked to intransience. If strong, value-laden world views are held then the perceptual changes will occur within those world view frameworks. Radical learning and the resultant radical change takes a major effort to achieve. The need to challenge those world views in a way that is non-threatening and appears to make sense to those in the situation is the way to approach the issue of creating change in the situation.

Change occurs constantly but it is relevant change which is important. Relevancy is a difficult issue because it implies that there is a good and a bad form of change according to different viewpoints and different needs. The ethics of change are central to any methodology which attempts to tackle real world situations. Even the principles of a methodology have an implied ethic and practice pulls in far more than just implication. In soft systems methodology the distinction is made between endemic change and purposeful change. This is the distinction between change which just occurs, irrespective of any intentionality of human intervention, and change which occurs because those involved in the situation see some point to the change. The emergent ethic of the methodology is that change is necessary because problem situations are undesirable and change that is purposefully enacted is more effective than change which is accidental, although the two are bound to be closely connected. The view of change explicit in the methodology is that it can and should be acted upon. Soft systems methodology is not to be used solely as a form of participant observation, although the use of the techniques associated with that school of thought are adopted within the methodology to help understanding of the situation. The methodology does not just ask those who use it to observe, it also demands that active intervention for purposeful change management occurs. This puts a greater onus on the user of the methodology as she/he cannot take a back seat in the problem situation. Involvement in that situation demands purposefully seeking to change it.

Action

The methodology is merely an intellectual curiosity if it is not being used to try to change the problem situation by improving it. Action is central to the methodology. The development of this methodology occurred through action research, and this is the mode in which it is constantly researched. Action is taken very seriously because it is the guiding force of the methodology. All the previous activities which have been discussed have all been for the purpose of leading up to action with the aim of improving the situation. The issue that needs addressing is concerned with what forms of action are implied by the methodology. We have already discussed above that purposeful action is important, that is, that the user of the methodology must act with the intention of seeking to find ways of improving the situation. This leads to a series of questions. Who is/are the user(s) of the methodology? If there is more than one, are there any conflicts of intention and, if so, how are they to be dealt with? Whose view of improving the situation is to be taken? How are conflicts in those views to be dealt with?

These questions need to be addressed by asking about the fundamental purpose of the methodology.

The methodology is intended for the creation of change by enhancing the dialectical process of the debate. Dialectics are the form of using opposition to get to a new accommodated view. This is referred to as thesis, antithesis, and synthesis, and is a form of Singerian inquiring systems as discussed by Churchman in his 1973 book *The Design of Inquiring Systems*. Checkland (1981) spends a great deal of time discussing the dialectical nature of action-based change implicit within the methodology. Viewing the situational traps is just the starting process (thesis). The opposite form is then looked at (antithesis). From the comparison a new view of the situation can emerge (synthesis). This use of different views allows for debate to occur by looking at the models of thesis, antithesis and the forming of synthesis. This is a rational view of change and hinges on the view that it is possible to have a world of open debate. Many sociologists have disagreed with this view and there have been criticisms of the methodology because of this rationality. The principles cannot be meaningfully criticized for this. It is acceptable to say that in principle there could be a world of open debate in which opposites are explored to create new visions. Plato developed the notion of the academy from this principle and universities, consortiums, councils, and even parliaments have been developed using similar principles. The practice may get messier but the principles are sound. However, practice needs to be more fully understood and criticisms answered if principles are to be worthy of anything more than rhetoric.

Another theoretical set of principles is adopted by soft systems methodology. This is developed from Vickers' concept of the appreciative system which was introduced in chapter 3. Vickers argues that we can explain the process of decision-making, which all humans take part in, by using systems ideas. We are all developing by appreciating perceptions and points of view. The way in which we incorporate these into our own viewpoints can be described as an appreciative system. We make judgements depending upon past prejudices and present interpretations of experiences. This leads to a judgemental framework through which decisions are made. This is how we make sense of the flux of the world of everyday experiences. We construct our appreciative setting by selecting what is relevant to us in this everyday flux and we continue to view future considerations from this constructed appreciative setting. The act of appreciating leads to changes in our interpretation of the setting and this involves changes in the framework, or appreciative system. It is impossible to perceive, judge, decide and act upon the flux without reference to this appreciative system. The process of change is always bounded by where it has developed to at the time of the new experiences. In this way, the appreciative system is both the necessary apparatus for enabling judgements in the complexity of the flux of the world of everyday life, and also the perceptual and judgemental trap which we view everything through. We need a process of debate with others to help revise our appreciative system and see our trap. But we are always constrained because we enter that debate through the use of the appreciative system and so only perceive others and their views from that viewpoint.

This seems an impossible trap but it is not. Just as the appreciative system is constraining, it is also fluid and capable of constant change. It does not demand revolutionary change in which the system of appreciation is overthrown. That form of change would be impossible from Vickers' stance because change must come from within and cannot simply wholly seek to replace views already existing. Radical change is only accomplishable through challenging of the appreciative system from within its bounded views. The dialectic must aim to change from within rather than by overthrowing and replacing. The form of change which Vickers talks of is accommodation. This demands an assimilation of views into the existing framework whilst seeking to move some of the more transient aspects of those views. In any human social situation there are many alternative views possible. Some situations are constraining and demand conformity so that a dominant view is protected. Any anarchic responses to that view are socially prevented from entering the arena of the debate. What is needed is an appreciative setting in which alternative views can be put forward without fear of repression from conformity inducement. This is an ideal type world. It is fundamental to the principles of the methodology that it should be approached as a purposeful aim when using the methodology. The aim is to develop a communication setting which will allow for the process of accommodation of different views to take place. This makes the boundaries of various traps more opaque and fluid. The traps can be viewed and discussed by the discussion of alternatives. Different views can then be perceived. This is the first requirement if change to the views is to be possible. The aim is not to start off with one view of what the ideal change should be and then to seek to indoctrinate those in the situation with this view, but to allow discussion of the different views so as to nurture the formation of an emergent view from which those who hold the other views feel it is possible to communicate with each other. This means that the outcome of the use of the methodology cannot be designed at the start. All that can be designed, using that term in its broadest sense, is the situation which can allow for accommodation of different views to be heard. This is what is meant by using the methodology to structure the debate.

The methodological principles argue that the structuring of the debate should develop and use systems models. This use states that a variety of different theoretical world views can be modelled. These are the Weltanschauungen found in all conceptual models. Each model expresses only one world view which is an ideal type, that is, it is not a world view which is necessarily held by anyone in particular (or at all) within a situation. The actions logically associated with that world view are made apparent by the development of a human activity system model to express this. It is then that those actions are compared with the problem situation so that the consequences of adopting that world view in the real world of the problem situation are seen. Prejudicial judgemental frameworks and consequential actions are made visible. The purpose of doing this is to allow for the rationality of the debate to provide enlightenment so that choices regarding changes to action can be considered. This is the principle for action-based change which is central to the methodology.

In principle, this structuring out of the logical consequences of actions associated with different world views should allow for a debate to ensue in which different changes can be considered, and this leads to different perceptions and accommodated viewpoints. Even though those in the problem situation may ultimately agree to fundamentally disagree, they can come to an accommodated view of how to act to make that situation less problematical for those involved in it. Conflict can be resolved by rationality and a desire to take action to change the situation. This principle holds the inherent view that people do not wish to live in constant opposition but are willing to act in a manner which will allow them to be together (or intentionally decide to part) even if deeply-held values are in opposition. We have all had experiences of having to work with people whose political and ideological statements are abhorrent to us, but we "put away personalities" and get on with the job. That is fine when we can visualize the actions required for the job and are not constrained by the value clashes and personalities. The methodology, in principle, aims to overcome the problems of ignorance of consequences and, in doing so, create both an appreciative setting in which different viewpoints can be accommodated, and actions to improve the situation which are both desirable and feasible. It aims to create an open environment for learning and appreciation so that the rationality of the dialectics of debate is made possible.

This is the fundamental ideal of the methodology. There are processes which can be adopted to try to create that ideal. These processes aim at enhancing communication, and allowing the occurrence of learning and appreciation. Many activities prevent learning by stopping disclosure and forcing conformity. Many social activities are oppressive and make communication a difficult task. Some approaches to change seek to heighten that model of oppression, exposing an implicit belief that there are forms of oppressors and oppressed within societies and that these should be radically shifted to favour the oppressed. This is not the belief inherent within soft systems methodology. Oppression is viewed as relative and inferential. It is a world view which needs challenging within the principles of approaches which accept it in a taken-for-granted format. Oppression is another of the perceptual traps which stop communication and needs exposing as a world view rather than as an ethical ideal to be protected at all costs. Rationality is the only assumption within the methodology which is fundamentally unchallenged.

Having clarified what the assumptions are in the principles of the methodology, we can now look at approaches to enhancing the principles. The key purpose of the methodology is to help debate. Open communication is a crucial belief. There are various approaches to help this process and some of them are strongly preferred in the later versions of the methodology. There is one prevalent view of methodologies, which is that they are tools to be used by skilled craftsmen, who then become the experts in producing the knowledge by using these tools. Anyone who adopts this view may not attempt to introduce the methodology into the situation. Rather, they are likely to use the methodology and then import their own considerations about the situation back into it. This notion of the expert advisor is being challenged more readily since the realization has been championed that those within the situation are the ones who should be and can be responsible for dealing with their own changes. One alternative to the view of the expert analyst and advisor is that of those within the situation learning their own way out of the situation. This can be done by intuitive means or with the help of some form of guide. A methodology provides a guide.

Participation

The view that those within the situation can and should be the ones to change it is attributed to a concept called participation. Enid Mumford has been a pioneer of participative information systems design and points out that there are three forms of participation, these being consultative, representative, and consensual. Mumford developed an approach to information systems design and development called ETHICS, an acronym standing for Effective Technical and Human Implementation of Computer-based work Systems. This methodology can be described as a soft systems approach to information management in relation to information systems design, development, and implementation. ETHICS is arguably a soft systems approach because it takes as paramount the human aspects of systems. It is a socio-technical systems approach as is soft systems methodology. Human systems are the subject of concern for Mumford as they are for Checkland, though in a different perspective. However, these differences are more theoretical than pragmatic and many of the issues regarding practice are shared by both Mumford and Checkland.

Mumford argues with conviction that there is an ethical aspect to the design of information systems and argues that those who do the jobs which are to be supported by computers are the best equipped to design the new work systems which include the use of computers. She also argues that they must be involved because there is an ethical need to get those who do the jobs to design their own jobs. Ownership of the task should start at the design stage and that should include control by future users. She has uncovered a number of benefits to a participative approach to any form of planned change.

Participation allows that knowledge of those who do the job can be directly used to improve the job. It also allows for those who are designing the tools of change, such as computers, to learn directly about the nature of work from those who do that work. It also means that communication between the technical designers and the users is enhanced as different beliefs and viewpoints are uncovered and a process of accommodation unfolds. Participation also ensures that those, who are to be involved in the new future resulting from the changes, are committed to it because they have been major contributors to the developments. Also, participation ensures that those who do the work can critically assess that work and deal with necessary changes which can improve the work. Finally, the ethical stance is that whoever does the work owns that work and so should be given the right to design it. The role of the user of the methodology then changes. The users must be those who are doing the change developments. Any form of expertise regarding the methodology must be passed on. The one who has been invited into the situation because she/he has some past knowledge of a methodology is then primarily concerned that those who wish to use it can take on board what they require from the methodology. This means that the methodology is no longer sacrosanct. It will change according to the needs of the people adopting it in that situation. The introducing user must not be over-psychologically attached to it but would do better to look at the variation that it can produce in use as opposed to in theory.

There are many problems with participation. The greatest issue is that it is often viewed as disruptive to everyday organizational practices. It involves stopping people from just doing their own work in their own sections, and getting together people from different sections to talk to each other about their work and about how they necessarily have to interact in order to perform the processes of that work. Many managers have got so used to having solutions presented to them by experts in the form of reports which they can take home and read, that they balk at the thought of internally developed solutions with workers thinking about their jobs instead of just doing them! This is a general cultural model of organizational problem-solving which is widespread. Some organizations have listened in part to the arguments regarding the benefits and have tried out participation, not realizing how much time and effort is required to make it work. It is then dismissed as too costly and not presenting immediate and obvious results. When organizational learning is the basis of change it is difficult to see quick and easy solutions enacted. However, there are now many instances of participation that have worked (see, for example, Mumford and Macdonald (1989) which is mentioned in the readings section at the end of this chapter).

Realizing the problems with the organizational prejudices regarding participation, Mumford has argued for three forms of participation. These forms differ in the distance they see between the users and their direct involvement in the development process of any planned change. The most distant is that of consultative participation. This is where one or more individuals becomes the spokesperson(s) for those involved in the change situation. Any change considerations are formed as part of a debate which is structured around the interpretations of the spokespersons. They will consult with those who are involved in the situation, that is, those who are recognized as stakeholders to any form of change. The purpose of consultation is to gather a combined view of what the issues are and what needs to be done about them. Whoever is in the consultative role is bound by the need to consider others' views throughout the process of change. The consultant is not an expert but a medium and facilitator of communication for those with the concerns. The difference is as much one of attitude as one of behaviour. This form of consultant has to ask themselves constantly whether or not they are still representing the various views when they consider alternatives and discuss the various possible changes. It demands an active openness of mind and continual self-reflection. It is difficult to keep check on whether the consultant is acting in this manner. Also, it is very difficult for the consultative participator to deal with many conflicting viewpoints. There is a strong possibility that this form of participation can lead to political game playing and the use of the consultant as a pawn. Consultative participation often means that a consultant is chosen by some power source and treated with distrust by those who feel they could be abused by that power source.

The next form of participation is that of representative participation. Here a representative is chosen to present the views of each group of individuals at any forum where change options are discussed. These representatives would be free to act in line with their own judgements, but would have to be sure that those judgements do represent the views required. This form of participation is a result of the stakeholders giving their power to participate to one or more selected individuals who are then left with the responsibility to represent their views. This is a form of democracy by nomination. One problem with this is the way that the nomination occurs. If the stakeholders are left to vote for their chosen representative then it is possible that a popular individual will be chosen rather than someone best suited to doing the job. If the representative is chosen by one or more of the interest groups then they can be perceived by other interest groups to be biased. The problems associated with conflict management and dealing with divergent views, which were discussed above in regard to the consultant, also hold for the representative. Even with these issues, the representative approach is often used. This is usually out of necessity. If large groups of people are to be affected by the changes then it is necessary to get the design group down to a manageable membership. This means that representation or consultation has to be relied upon. However, many of the communication benefits can be lost if the information is not passed backwards and forwards in a group-oriented, structured manner. It is possible to use multiple representation as a way to ensure participation. This means setting up a series of groups, with representatives from each moving between groups, where change-related information is discussed and action plans are set. In this way there is diffusion of the necessary learning for effective change operationalized throughout the organization.

The final form of participation is that of consensus participation. This is where the number of stakeholders in the change situation is small enough, and the scope of the problem is contained enough, to allow for all of them to be present throughout the learning and action phases. This form of participation has many benefits so long as the group processes are accounted for. The working group which comes together will continue to work together after the project and so enhanced working relationships can occur. Communication is easier because the people are more continually involved. The commitment is more dependable because the people are constantly involved both in their own futures and in those of their working colleagues. The application of an elementary understanding of group processes and a determination to keep the group self-reflective and open is needed to make these groups work. Concentration on task allows for process management and the commitment allows for motivation. Most people enjoy being involved in their own jobs! The problems occur when there is conflict between different interest groups within the group, as can happen when problem situations are being addressed. The need for managing an openness of communication and supporting a desire for accommodation is paramount. The metaphor of a methodology provides a process framework to allow for this, and the models generated provide a forum for debate which is less threatening than direct personal confrontation.

As previously mentioned, despite the benefits of participation many organizations are reluctant to adopt the approach. When a methodology espouses the need for a participative approach to its use, as is the case with soft systems methodology, then consultative participation may be the only one of the three possibilities available. To move away from talking about the methodology hypothetically, we will now move back to the study presented in chapter 2 to look at the use of the methodology.

The use of the methodology

Throughout this book a clear distinction has been made between what the principles of a methodology imply should happen and what the practice of using that methodology states does happen. It is a problem with every methodology that it is virtually impossible to evaluate a methodology. This is because a methodology is only a set of guidelines for action. Every use is simply an idiosyncratic example of one application of those principles as interpreted by the user(s) on that particular occasion. If the situation does not work out then it could be because the users were incapable of applying the principles well enough or it could be because the methodology itself was inadequate or inappropriate. The same applies if success is attributed to the occasion of use. It could just be that the talents of the user caused success and little or nothing to do with the methodology. Any user is far richer and more complicated than any set of principles called a methodology. A further problem is that it is not always obvious what measures of performance are being applied to the use, so it is uncertain as to what exactly a success or a failure would be. However, general lessons can be learned from using a methodology. Reflective experiences of practice help to uncover the metaphorical aspects of the guidelines when placed against their practical application in a given situation.

Most written accounts of the use of a methodology tend to over-rationalize that use. We see the principles being adhered to and the framework of the metaphor of the methodology being talked through. That is because of cultural expectations regarding the reporting of what are called 'studies', be they termed 'case studies' or 'field studies'. However, there is a growing body of literature which aims to separate the rhetoric of the methodology from the reflection on the action. Telling it like it happened, or at least like it appeared to happen, is becoming a more acceptable option. In the illustrative study, the experience is reported through the framework of the methodology. The use of that methodology is played down. In this chapter that use comes to the fore and is delved into so that some of the issues regarding using a methodology to enhance action for change can be looked at. The study is far from perfect (whatever that may be!) but it is educative. As the purpose of this book is primarily to educate, then the study can at least be adopted for its utility value.

Revisiting the rhetoric: the problem situation

The situation of the Army example is contrived to some extent because it is part of a doctoral thesis. This is why it is a study rather than just an experience. Every reported action has some degree of contrivance. It is worth looking at that contrivance to ask how initiation occurred. This is important because it shows the first interpretive framework to which the user of the methodology is operating.

The following section refers back to the study, and so we return to first person reporting.

The study was initiated in 1986. At that time, talk of soft systems methodology being primarily participatory was rare. The developers of the methodology, particularly the Lancaster group, were carrying on with the exploration of the methodology that had been continuing for nearly twenty years. Over that time the methodology had changed forms and focus in many ways. This transient nature of any methodology makes the study of it very difficult! When the study was first started I had recently been an undergraduate in Systems at Lancaster and had experienced the rarefied atmosphere of carrying out theoretical work on the concept of *Weltanschauung* in soft systems methodology as an independent studies student working with Peter Checkland. That had a deep effect on my beliefs about the concept called soft systems methodology. At the time of the Army study I was on the doctoral programme at Manchester Business School working under the supervision of Enid Mumford, so I had a great deal of contact with ideas on participation. I was at that awful stage in my doctoral work where I had done one study and was completely uncertain as to what my doctorate was about. (To let a trade secret out, when students know what their doctorates are about, they have finished and ought to be writing up their dissertations!) Although I was working with Enid, I was still doing soft systems methodology work. She knew this but I did not, and so I entered this study to use the methodology believing that I was looking at organizational culture and doing an ethnography. I had not yet come to realize what action research really is (if I ever did finish that journey of discovery).

When I was looking for this study I was very aware of the extreme difficulties of entering any organization to conduct essentially qualitative research work. I wanted a situation, any situation, at any cost. This leads to rampant opportunism being at the forefront of all judgements. At this time my husband, (the co-author) was a lecturer at the military college, and I was in social contact with military staff and officers. An opportunity arose and a kind-hearted soul could see some use in what I was looking at, if it was applied to his area of concern. This was the strategic development of computing in the Army. We had some preliminary discussions and he directed me towards certain documents, one of which was the strategy report. After some further discussions we decided that it would be worthwhile if I looked at the strategy and carried out some form of evaluation to see if problems with it could be found, particularly by looking for issues of organizational behaviour. This was to allow me to start on a longer process of looking at the organizational culture and prepare me for taking part in a much larger project with a team of people at a later date. It was intended to be a preliminary and minor study. It was also seen as unnecessary to go through all the formal procedures of clearing my project with higher authorities. I had signed the Official Secrets Act so I had the minimum necessary clearance to look at some documents and visit some buildings. As I very soon took on part-time lecturing at the military college I also went through a very minor checking procedure called 'negative vetting'. I had entered through a back door with a champion/informant and neither of us envisaged that I would have any problems with this.

The methodology was a useful framework at first, in that it directed me to look for a problem situation using the forms of analysis discussed in chapter 3. At that time the three forms of analysis were not so clearly represented in the literature and I had to rely on discussions about them with various people. Luckily one of these individuals was Checkland. I thought that the guidelines for the analysis of culture were far too sparse and so set about adding ideas from ethnography and anthropology. I did not realize it at the time but that was to be the main aspect of my doctoral work. I gathered information from a variety of sources as to what the Army was like. This included formal reports and written histories, formal and informal interviews, listening to gossip, attending ceremonies, and joining in social occasions. For six months I carried out a detailed ethnography whilst I 'waited' for my 'real' project to start. I was also greatly influenced by the anthropologist Clifford Geertz and kept a diary in which I was honest and searching in regard of my interpretation of, and feelings about, the Army. On reflection, it was probably, singularly, the most useful action in the entire study. I learnt a great deal about discovering a problem situation by becoming part of it in ways that I had not prepared myself for.

Doing a cultural analysis of the problem situation: pain and discovery

Doing action-based studies which demand involvement in human situations changes people. We are not just passive recorders but do become involved and sometimes that involvement is painful and traumatic. When I started this study I was willing to get involved because I just wanted to get on with my research. I felt a sense of commitment because I had agreed to adopt an action-based approach to looking at the situation; that is the approach of soft systems methodology. I felt responsible for my own actions as I was intending to seek to take action to improve something, I knew not what. I felt that some form of psychological contract had been entered into and that I had obligations to this organization. I had expected that some form of reciprocal caring would follow as, after all, I was told to expect a sense of participation between those in the situation and those trying to help. The individuals I came across in the Army were people exemplary in the social graces. I was cajoled into feeling a sense of importance about them, and a certain level of seduction occurred in that I started to value the organization and hold it in high esteem. This was, at first, strange to me as a pacifist. I reconciled the conflict by telling myself that the primary purpose of the Army was to manage peace. Later, on more than one occasion, I was told that that was a naive view and that preparation for war was much closer to the truth. By that time I was very involved and felt many moral conflicts between caring for the organization and the people I met, and I felt a sense of abhorrence that the primary activities were geared towards killing others. Every situation has a sense of the political, and no methodology warns you of the personal conflicts, nor does it guide you in how to cope with them.

As I started into the study, I visited many staff and field posts. I was very conscious of being a woman, mainly because it was constantly referred to, and because I met so few other women. I met one woman 'squaddie' who was my driver on one occasion and she told me that she was leaving the Army because it was "no place for a woman". She told me that she was leaving to marry another soldier and by that time I knew enough to doubt that she would actually be truly leaving. I met one female officer who was one of my students who resorted to some strange behaviour on one occasion to get her fellow students' attention. I remarked on this and her response was "You know it is like that when you join. You either conform or get out". The problem is that not only am I female but I am something of a feminist. I found much of the behaviour very hard to accept.

I suffered some severe traumas during the study. These included a very painful gender crisis, moral dilemmas, inabilities to deal with conflicts between people's behaviour to me as an individual and their behaviour to me as a non-Army person, and identity problems concerning whether I was an insider to the organization or an outsider. I turned to the methodology to look for help in dealing with these problems. There is nothing there. I was confusing an idealized type metaphor, which is just a set of principles to guide actions, with expectations of a personal guide to carry me through all the difficult situations.

I discovered a problem situation and managed to get a great deal of material to support a cultural interpretation of that situation. I had done this from a stance which I was led into during the study, albeit implicitly rather than intentionally. I was seen as a wife and so introduced to the wives and their problems. I decided to tussle with my initial feelings, that this was not the best path to go along, and accept that any path is useful as it helps discovery and learning. I had carried on alone, with some regular contact with the individual who had first offered me the study. I worked hard by using the self-reflective medium of the diary to avoid acting as the expert overseer and I genuinely believed that I was trying to act through consultative participation. The main problem was that it was extremely difficult to identify the stakeholders in any firm sense, so I took those who expressed that there was a problem situation to be the stakeholders. The notion of problem owner seems to be far more useful than that of stakeholder. This meant that the problem owners were principally the wives, and their husbands who were the officers, particularly those involved in the course which developed them as information managers. However, wherever I went, even with people who had never been near the course, I continually heard about the eroding of the support for the family and the threat of breakdown of marriage alongside the dissatisfaction with the office-centred work roles.

I continued gathering information and feeding it back to whoever was interested and relevant, but particularly back to the initiator whom I had reconsidered as a decision taker as well as one of the many problem owners. On reflection, I did not consider this role deeply enough. I had assumed power and authority in that individual and that there would not be other decision takers who could, and would, override him. I gave the role away too easily without thinking about my relationship as problem solver. I also did not think hard enough about the notional problem solver. I had adopted the role whilst I needed to get others involved in that role. This was particularly important for this organization, because the Army is a highly formalized organization with very clear lines of demarcation between members and non-members. I was assuming that I could act as a member, because in some organizations this is not only possible but actively encouraged. I misread behaviour and thought that I would be able to help with the consideration of action to improve the problem situation without asking whether I had the political or formal influence to do that. There is a great deal to be gained from reflection upon the roles of problem owner, problem solver, and decision taker and I had treated these reflections far too trivially.

Modelling

A great deal is spoken of and written about in relation to the formal techniques of modelling in soft systems methodology. This may well give the false impression that this is the most important aspect of the methodology. It is not, it is just the safest, because it is the most firmly understood. However, I did at least resist the temptation to rush quickly into modelling and believe that I had a grasp of the problem situation. By the time I started dealing with the naming of relevant systems I was very deeply involved in the issues of the situation and grateful for the distancing that the formality of modelling allowed me. This is one major strength of the methodology. When the complexity of the situation becomes overwhelming, the rigour of having to sort out ideas and look to modelling can help the user to get out of the trap of that complexity. Although the principles of the methodology do not state this, it seems to me that in the use of the methodology this is a much underrated way of purposefully using modelling!

The relevant systems that were named were all very directly related to what was being expressed as the perception of the problem situation. When I developed the 'key personnel shortage maintaining system' I worked in the honest good faith that I was modelling an ideal type model and tried hard not to introduce thinking about the real world of the problem situation. I cannot know whether I achieved this or not. It is virtually impossible not to have ideas of the real world in your head when modelling. This guideline provides a lot of issues. I take it to mean that the construction of the root definition and the conceptual model should be logically whole and all the activities should only be those necessitated by the idea of a system which carries out the actions named in the identification of that system. It is during the consideration of the logical wholeness of that definition and model that thinking about what exists in the real world of known events should be avoided. Asking "can I do this activity directly before this one, or is there an activity missing?" can only be answered by some reference to both the logic of argument and an ideal model of what the logical flow of activities ought to be in this kind of system. All experience has been related to the real world at some point, so this delineation is not as absolute as would be convenient. However, despite these issues, I sought to close myself off from consideration of the real world as I was then experiencing it, and to stay with considerations regarding the logic of the system as a whole entity. That is what I take to be the use of the principle of developing models in the world of systems thinking rather than in the real world of the problem situation.

It is an obvious criticism that the named relevant systems were all very close to the interpretation of the problem situation. The one which is shown in chapter 2 seems to express what appeared to me to be a central issue in that situation. As I was not passing the modelling on but using it to help me to learn so that I could communicate my learning to others, I was happy with using the modelling in this form. It may have been useful to have worked directly in the dialectic form and to have also developed a model of 'A key personnel quota maintaining system', but I did not. At the time I did not think of this alternative, although thinking in the dialectic should have helped me to do that. In any use of a methodology it is easy to be wise with hindsight, and whilst in the muddle of the situation it is difficult to check that all the alternatives offered by the methodology have been tried out.

The learning gained from comparison was extremely useful for me and I saw many things that my confusion had previously not allowed me to see. These are discussed in greater detail in chapter 2. Comparison is the heart of the use of the methodology. It is in doing this action that learning is most rigorously unfolded. I was learning that the model of the 'key personnel shortage maintaining system' had many strong comparisons with actions in the situation. The actions appeared rational, logical, and unchallengeable to those in the situation because they supported firm beliefs and values associated with cultural biases. In the language of the methodology they were systemically desirable because they matched the logic of the system model, and they were culturally feasible because they made sense in the cultural framework through which the organization was seeing the world. The problem seemed to be that cultural purposes were at odds with everyday working purposes. The culture was being eroded and some of the norms were shown to be threatening to the existence of the organization. Yet it was this very strength of the culture that held the organization together when there were severe problems. The culture was itself problematical. This meant that being culturally feasible was not necessarily a good thing. It is not immediately obvious that the methodology provides guidance for this kind of situation where cultural changes had to be debated, but it does. It seems that another problem situation had unfolded and further use of the methodology was required by going back to the starting phases and iterating in order to explore this newly found issue.

The study had the same problem as all attempts at dealing with problem situations. Time was running out. I was expected to deliver something that could be used by person or persons unknown. I had tried to give feedback along the line of the use of the methodology to date, and to involve those who were recognized as problem owners throughout the learning process. I had already discovered a great deal about the problem situation from the use of SSM. The problem was that I was largely discovering it alone. I was involving those with whom I had contact, as best as the situation would allow me to, and they were an important part of the problem situation. These were in part the wives groups who were involved in trying to get a hearing regarding the erosion of family support. These people had been involved with some of my learning, as had the officers I had interacted with. The gravest mistake which I made was in not questioning who really would have the authoritative power to adopt the role of decision taker. I had gone through a voyage of discovery and tried to keep those travelling with me as informed as I could. I had bounded my frame for the appreciative setting around them. I had ignored the unseen, unknown authorities who also wanted results, mainly because I had not been directed to think of them in any significant way. I had to write a report which would have a wider audience than that of the appreciative setting which I had bounded. I had mapped my journey along paths which were too narrow. Most importantly, the process of my voyage of discovery was not shared by those I was later to write a report for. This proved problematical for the consideration of the closure of this study and is discussed in the next section.

Action, change and exit

Soft systems methodology demands that the user take action to improve the problem situation. The crucial consideration is that of who is designated user and how he or she is likely to be able to take action. I have gone into some detail regarding how this project was initiated. It is important because initiation should be linked to considerations of closure. That is what researching the use of soft systems methodology has taught me. The initiation was with the expectation that the study would be fairly minor and trivial. It was really intended to be a filler until the real project could be started. Because of this, there were no formal procedures carried out to clear my entry into the study, but those who were receiving the report were those who should have been formally approached. It was necessary for them to receive it so that they could be more formally approached for the next study. It was expected that the findings of this study would be fairly innocuous and that the report would, therefore, be merely an exercise, and not expected to have any real effect on the situation. I was not really taking this into account as I was adopting the stance of the methodology and, having found a problem situation, was attempting to take action to change it. In the report I simply talked through the comparison, using simple and straight-forward language to explain the problem situation and how a shortage in key personnel was going to threaten the operationalization of the strategy. The report was only five pages long and the only recommendations were that a task force look at the family issues and that some form of insignia was allowed for members of the IT training course so that they could feel that their new knowledge was significant to the organization. The report was sent to my initiator who read it and contacted me to say that he was happy with it and was sending it on to those whom he felt should be reading it. He said that he would be in contact soon regarding the next study and we had some discussions about what this was going to be. It sounded exciting and I felt very pleased. I heard nothing for a few weeks, but realized that this is normal as starting new organizational studies takes time and demands patience. Meanwhile, I continued to work on the data I had accrued regarding the culture of the Army and continued to lecture at the military college where I was considering taking up a full-time post. My professor who headed the department was an ex-officer in the Army and had given me a great deal of information. We had a good working relationship. One day he called me into his office and told me that he had some bad news. He had just had a phone call simply saying "Lynda Davies must not enter any Ministry of Defence buildings". All access had been stopped, quickly, absolutely, and without warning. I was shattered by the experience. The professor told me that the military college was a Ministry of Defence building, but as I was employed by the college I was not just to be turfed out. However, he had been concerned for security reasons and so checked out why this action had been taken. Had I not been something of an insider I would not have had this privilege. He informed me that I was not a security risk, but a sensitivity risk. That was all the information he would disclose. It meant that I could go on working at the college but not go on researching the Army. Shortly after that I was contacted by the officer who had initiated the study who asked me to visit the venue for the next study to discuss it, as he was trying to get me reinstated. I was grateful and went. It looked like a marvellous project to be involved in and I would be acting as part of a team. The day after that visit I was contacted again and told that I was definitely out. I gave up all hopes of continuing with a further study in that organization and looked elsewhere. However, I did not cease lecturing at the military college and took up a full-time post. It was many months later that I came to see the effects of the study. A revised strategy was written and, being at the college, I had access to it. It had two additions, these being the two recommendations which I made. I felt some sense of satisfaction. Later, I was dining in mess with the officer who had been the initiator when he told me that the main reason I had been stopped was because it was obvious from the report that I understood too much for an outsider. A methodology which helps to make visible the traps, can create further ones for the user! He also relayed the contents of the telephone call to me which had caused the cessation of my involvement in the follow-up study. The basic message was that my purpose was viewed as to help them to learn but they were not there to learn, they were there to work. Some cultures simply do not accept very easily the basic premises of some methodologies.

Success or failure?

This study has been presented in great detail for the purposes of helping users to learn the limitations of any methodology as well as the strengths. I know that the methodology helped me a great deal to make sense of a complex and difficult problem situation. In this way I think that the methodology was successful, as it stopped me going under in the confusion which a situation-based piece of action can provide. It gave me clarity of thought and of expression. That is witnessed by the response which indicated that I had seen things too clearly. The problems lay in the fact that I had largely discovered them alone. Had I been able to work in a more classically participative mode, as the follow-up study offered, I feel sure that the effects would not have been so dramatic. But change occurred, action to improve the problem situation had taken place so I cannot say that everything failed.

The problem is that I cannot quite put my finger on what exactly succeeded either. Something did. It seems that the learning and the content of the message did succeed even if my intervention techniques did not. I learnt a great deal from that study. I still am learning. That is another element of the success.

I also learnt about the limitations of looking only to the principles of a methodology when guidance for action is needed. It is ridiculous to expect any generalizable methodology to be able to provide help and guidance for dealing with all the vast array of issues that occur in any real world context. The methodology provided a framework, a set of actions, and the strength of systems modelling. Like any good guide, it is wise to use it whilst also looking at the prevailing conditions and changes that occur during the duration of the trip. Use of the methodology will always have degrees of unpredictability and will always rely upon additional learning gained from coping with problem situations as well as learning regarding the techniques of the methodology.

Conclusions

Although this is not the final chapter of the book it is the last look in detail at soft systems methodology. It is unlikely that all the learning which is potentially available in this book will have been fully developed from the first journey through it. You, the reader, have been given our impressions on what the methodology is, what its principles and techniques are, how to develop them to a skilful level, and what at least one experience of using the methodology has entailed. It is hoped that the reading of the work will continue both by rereading aspects of this book and by extending the learning by use of the readings which are given at the end of each chapter. It is hoped that the exercises will continue to provide learning opportunities.

Having given a great deal of information on the methodology itself, and a number of learning opportunities, the final chapter summarizes the book by looking back to the opening discussion about the concept of information in action, to which soft systems methodology relates.

Discussion issues

1. This study was about an IT strategy in a large public sector organization and shows that human aspects of the organization can prevent effective implementation of a technology-related change. Discuss what the main issues are with the relationship between information technology changes and organizational behaviour as highlighted in this study. Do you think that the situation would have been any different if the organization had been in the private sector, although still large and old? Would it have been very different if it was manufacturing technology rather than information technology? How could you apply soft systems methodology to the exploration of your assumptions?

2. Why do you think that methodologies do not generally tell users how to act in different social problem situations?

3. What different approaches to entry and exit could have helped make this particular situation easier on the methodology user?

4. Are all change situations necessarily political? Does being an 'insider' to a situation make things easier or more difficult than being an 'outsider'?

5. What does this situation help you understand about the espoused role of the systems analyst? Is it possible to do systems analysis without getting involved in cultural, social and political tangles?

Exercises

1. Now that a detailed account of this study has been given, it is worthwhile to discuss some of the lessons which can be drawn from the study. See if you can name three key lessons in relation to the use of the methodology which have not already been covered.

2. Develop the root definition and conceptual model of the "key personnel quota maintaining system". Compare it with the model of the "key personnel shortage maintaining system" given in chapter 2. What have you learned about possible changes to the problem situation from this comparison?

3. Do a root definition, CATWOE analysis, conceptual model, and comparison of a "System to manage change in political situations" which can then be put against the account of the study in this chapter. Can you find ways to help manage the change process from this?

4. From your model, which you developed in exercise 3, look at how information could have been managed better to improve the change process.

5. Compare this chapter with chapter 2. From this comparison, see if you can create a root definition, CATWOE analysis, conceptual model, and comparison of a "System to use soft systems methodology". Compare your system with others. If they differ, try to understand why this may be so.

6. Acting as a consultant to the user of the methodology in this chapter, write a five page review and report, suggesting how managing information to help the learning process could be done differently. Make sure that you can justify what you are taking the learning process to be, as there may be many interpretations of this.

Suggested reading

Burgess, R. (ed), *In the Field: An introduction to field research*, Allen & Unwin, 1984.

This is a useful book to see what any work which deals with human situations has to contend with. It is to help those dealing with ethnographies but is equally applicable to those learning to deal with problem situations.

Rosenhead, J. (ed), *Rational Analysis in a Problematic World*, Wiley, Chichester, U.K., 1989.

This is an excellent set of readings in the area known as 'soft operational research'. It includes two chapters on soft systems methodology, one on the theory and one on practice. It discusses how human rational action is very different from the rational action expected of logical machines, which is the metaphor still implicitly held by many texts dealing with management science.

Checkland, P.B. & Scholes, J., *Soft Systems Methodology in Action*, Wiley, Chichester, UK, 1990.

Again this book is recommended. It is particularly useful for this chapter as the title suggests. The book shows how participation can be used in novel forms. A note from Checkland has him stating that he hopes the book:
"(a) shows what flexible use of SSM using technically credible models is like and
(b) changes the view of SSM away from the '7 stages' ideal type."
We believe that it succeeds on both accounts and urge the reader to turn to that book to understand more fully the lessons which this book has tried to put forward.

Mumford, E. and Macdonald, W.B., *XSEL's progress: the continuing journey of an expert system*, Wiley, Chichester, UK, 1989.

This is an excellent book on participation. It is a success story but it shows the trials and tribulations of carrying out an action-based project. It is a superb read!

8 Reflections on the learning process

- *Information and learning*
- *The role of the information manager*
- *Soft systems methodology and information management*
- *Information and problem situations*
- *Using formalized systems thinking*
- *Reflecting and learning*

By the time the reader has reached this part of the book, it is hoped that a great deal of learning about soft systems methodology has occurred. It is also hoped that the learning will not stop with reading through the book once, but will carry on and encourage the reader as learner to return to it. Soft systems methodology is a framework for understanding a learning process which is iterative in nature, that is, the path of the steps of the methodology can be returned to many times to take the learning journey again. This book is intended to be taken in the same light. The book has taken the reader through a great many new concepts, both in nature and in technique. Concepts do not enter the appreciative act without a continual reflection. It is hoped that the continual process of learning about the methodology in use and in theory will have started by now, but will not finish here. To help that iterative process, this final chapter reflects on the learning process which has been presented in the book.

Information and learning

In order to learn we must be able to perceive through a framework of enquiry. That demands making sense of the world about us. Sense-making is not possible if we cannot construct what is informative and what is not. Sense-making and information management are reciprocal creators. As we make sense of the chaos around us, so we create what we take to be informative, reject what is non-informative, and manage our newly formed information into an order with previously formed information. We reconstruct our world as a sensible place to live in. This reconstruction process is a meaning-creation exercise. We cannot have meaning unless we have some form of information. Learning is not possible if we cannot be informed, but learning also makes possible that information.

This process of intertwined learning, information creation and management is a continual process in our everyday lives. It is when the process breaks down that we experience distortion to our understanding, confusion, and the trauma of chaos. Humans wish to order their worlds. They strive to learn and to attribute meaning to their constructions of the world. Humans cannot do this without adopting an active perspective on information. This does not mean that they have to find information, but that the process of creating and managing information is inevitable with cognizant human beings. There is no way of creating a world which is not one of information.

This view of information in action is very different to the one which is constantly given in student textbooks. These other books give the impression that there are specialists who understand what information is and have technical means to analyze and capture that information which they then treat and store in a special way. They become specialized members of corporations whilst doing this. Very often they are technological specialists rather than information specialists. They support the context for information manipulation rather than the necessary learning process of information management. There is no reason why they cannot do both.

The role of the information manager

If we take the view that information and learning are contingent and that we cannot prevent information creation and management from occurring, we look at the role of the information manager in a very different light than it being primarily that of technology manager. The role of the information manager becomes less concerned with technical specifications and more concerned with understanding and explicating the information which is currently most salient for the organization. They must have the ability to make explicit the frameworks for making sense of the world which members of the organization are most dependent on. They must learn to understand the organization through its members' appreciative frameworks. They must also be able to perceive the potential traps of thinking and help to work within the appreciative frameworks and to help renegotiate the reality, so that the traps are avoided, or at least prevented from becoming chaotic. They must be capable of being information actors. The role of this kind of information manager is far more demanding. It is that of the wise sage, the keeper at the gates of sanity, and also of the champion for change. It is rather like that of the master to whom the novice turns for guidance, but who provides it by standing by during the learning process and probing the ideas of the learner to create reflection. In this way the master becomes the learner and the learning journey becomes a sharing of the creation of wisdom.

This interpretation of the role of information manager is not only far more demanding but it is also not necessarily given to specialized members of any organization. Because it is a role, it is something that any member can take up at any time. The point is that information managers should primarily view themselves as guiders of the learning process of sense-making. The aim of information in action is to help make that guidance more explicit by supporting it with useful frameworks for enquiry. Anyone and everyone is an information actor all the time. Whether they set out explicitly to improve that process is the key question. If that is the aim then ways of helping to improve the process of learning, enquiry, sense-making and reconstruction of information is what is required to support the role of the information manager.

Soft systems methodology and information management

Soft systems methodology is a framework for helping to make sense of the process of learning in social situations. The sense-making includes ordering that learning process in a formal manner. As the sense-making process is a process whereby information is created and managed, any framework for aiding that process must be a framework for supporting and enhancing information management. The more explicit the processes of that framework, the easier it becomes to make explicit the information management processes to which it can be applied. To help information management as an explicated form of sense-making, methodologies are needed to explicate the learning process. That is the fundamental process of soft systems methodology. To understand how soft systems methodology provides a framework for managing information as a learning process, it is helpful to reflect back through the book and look at what the methodology has offered.

Information and problem situations

Soft systems methodology makes explicit the belief that situations are what become problematical and this is often because of conflicts in perceptions, interests, or strategies, as well as because of differing degrees of a lack of appreciation of others' viewpoints. Because situations are social constructs which are continually renegotiated, it is in the social management of meaning that problems can occur. This is often unintentional, but may be an intentional act by people who wish to disrupt the current sense-making framework and replace it with one in which they feel that they can more easily dominate. This is where political views of information and sense-making come to the fore.

In this book, the initial approach to the methodology is first to look at the problem situation and to ask questions about how it arose. This means understanding key roles such as problem owner, decision taker and initiator. Once this has been looked at, the more fundamental analyses of the situation may begin. These look at culture, roles, values, and norms, and the power and politics of the situation. Culture is fundamental to the sense-making activities of any situation. It is through cultural frameworks that we understand the world by attributing meaning to events, acts, and objects. We create those frameworks through social actions which are historically bound and then become entrapped in them in our sense-making. They are the fundamental managers of information in social contexts in that they are the implicit frameworks that we all use to understand what is informative, and what is not, when we construct meanings. Using the cultural analyses which have been given in this book, those implicit frameworks can be more readily identified. This is a necessary first step if we are to explicate the information management processes already happening within any problem situation.

Because we are not merely absorbers of information but actively take part in the process of learning which is information creation and management, we sometimes try intentionally to control that process by seeking to control the social situation. This is the political view of information management. The methodology provides guidelines for recognizing the political aspects of the situation so that these can be explicated, challenged, or treated with caution. We can start to understand how commodities of learning can be used to become commodities of power. Information is treated as something which can be manipulated, withheld, or selectively given out so that power strategies can be played. The learning process becomes a negotiative arena where individuals, or groups, try to retain control of the process by controlling the creation and management of information. Influence becomes a key mover in this process. The methodology can provide help in recognizing this by making more explicit the dominant world views and how they may be being used as part of the political process of sense-making.

Using formalized systems thinking

To help with the activities of explicating and managing the learning process of information creation and management, more formalized approaches to modelling frameworks of enquiry are needed. Soft systems methodology provides these by presenting a rigorous and controlled approach to the modelling of human activity systems as ideal types. Chapters 3, 4 and 5 have gone into great detail to help develop the technical knowledge needed to do this well. Doing it poorly will only decrease the possibility of good explication, and subsequent good learning. This is why the book has concentrated in such detail on the technical aspects of the methodology. Without good technical knowledge, the user can become lost and confused. This is most definitely not the aim of the methodology, which is far more concerned with creating clarity to enhance learning.

Systems thinking is a particularly useful conceptual tool to help explication because it deals with interacting elements and emergent properties from those interactions, rather than dealing with issues in piecemeal form. There is segmentalization though, which comes from looking at different world views which are implicit in different systems models. This allows for activities and points of view to be defensibly associated together as idealized forms. These can then be compared with the views and actions in the problem situation so that learning can be enhanced. This enhancement occurs through making more explicit the implicit understanding of the situation which is already present. In this way, the models provide formalized accounts of information creation and managing activities which are ideally present so that the processes actually present can be understood. This allows for a renegotiation and subsequent further learning.

It is has been argued continuously throughout chapter 6, that the comparison of models with the situation as perceived is the most powerful and fundamental part of soft systems methodology. This is because it is at this point that the frameworks for sense-making in the problem situation become explicated. They are opened up for discussion and negotiation. It is here that the methodology provides a means of formally managing the sense-making process which is information creation and management. It is where learning occurs, not as a magical process but as an explicated process. We come to understand how the world is being understood through the questioning of the models. It is the period of enlightenment when the past sense-making is disclosed. Because of this enlightenment, it is also where new information management frameworks are created. It is in the truest form of explicated information management in the whole of the methodology. That is why everything that has gone before is simply carried out to support this later process of comparison. The learning derived, and the new information management frameworks can then be used to start the process again and to create new learning through renegotiation. Iteration becomes the basis of learning and of the management of information.

Reflecting and learning

Reading through the book leads the reader to reassess the initial study presented in the light of the consideration of the use of the methodology. We reflect upon what seemed to happen as a more confused social process (chapter 7) compared with how we understood the situation as a process through the methodology (chapter 2). This reflection then leads on to challenge how much we can really expect of any methodology as a guide for the learning process. We realize that a methodology is only a framework to guide action, it cannot dictate the action nor provide a full understanding of all actions. We need to become reflective learners to become fully capable of using this or any methodology.

Learning is what we do all the time. Reflection is what we need to become more explicitly competent. If we can manage that, then we become more intelligent managers of our information as we come to understand better our learning process. Soft systems methodology merely provides a useful and rigorous framework to support that reflective process. It is hoped that this book enhances that process by enhancing the learning needed in order to become a good user of the methodology, both technically and reflectively. This is the basic foundation required of becoming an Information Actor managing information as a learning process.

Discussion issues

1. Discuss whether it is possible to have learning which does not provide information.

2. Reflecting upon the methodology, does it seem feasible to look at models of human activity systems as models of information? If so, in what way? What view of information emerges from this?

3. Discuss what the role of 'information' technology has in the learning processes in any organization. How could the technology be better used to support that learning process?

Exercises

1. Develop a root definition and conceptual model of a 'system to manage information'. Compare the model with what has been argued in this chapter. What have you learnt about:
   (i) the methodology,
   (ii) the nature of information,
   (iii) the nature of information management, and
   (iv) the reflective process of learning?

2. Develop a rich picture of the learning process in this book. Name relevant systems which are relevant to enquiring into that learning process. From this learning, how would you improve the book?

Suggested reading

Galliers, R. (ed), *Information analysis: selected readings*, Addison-Wesley, Sydney, 1987.

This book provides useful readings which challenge the dominant technological view of information.

Hirschheim, R. A., *Office automation: a social and organizational perspective*, Wiley, Chichester, 1985.

The philosophy of Hirschheim's book is closely aligned to the notion of the management of information expressed in this book.

Index

accommodation 129, 137, 138, 140, 143

act of enquiry 134

action research 15, 135, 145

action-based change 136, 138

activity model 101, 114

activity system model 26, 72, 79, 86, 125, 138

actor 68, 71, 93, 160, 163

analytical 110, 111, 112

analytical form 9

analytical process 33

anthropology 43, 146

antithesis 136

appreciation 4, 30, 36, 38, 42, 51, 55, 56, 137, 139, 161

appreciative 19, 36, 40, 42-44, 51, 54, 136-138, 151, 158, 159

appreciative act 158

appreciative setting 19, 40, 42, 43, 54, 136-138, 151

appreciative system 36, 42, 51, 136, 137

army 15, 17-20, 25-28, 55, 127, 144-148, 152

artifacts 5, 6, 43

assimilation 129, 131, 137

attribute mapping 112, 122-125

authority 37, 47, 81, 146, 148, 151

Backhouse, J. 1, 8

behaviour(s) 3, 5, 17, 38-42, 45, 48, 50, 52, 128, 142, 146-148, 155

behavioural 45

boundary, -ies 16, 25, 41, 93, 94, 103, 123, 124, 137

Burgess, R. 156

CATWOE 12, 22, 23, 25, 53, 58, 63, 68, 70-72, 74, 78, 79, 81, 83, 87, 93, 94, 95, 97, 102, 103, 156

change 4, 12, 14, 16, 26, 28, 29, 33-43, 45, 46, 49-51, 61, 68, 69, 73, 76, 82, 96, 105,

108, 111, 121, 122, 127-129, 133-144, 151, 152, 153, 155, 156, 160

change
- feasible and desirable 12, 81, 97, 98, 100, 127, 133
- endemic 135
- instigator 26
- purposeful 121, 135

charisma 49

Checkland, P.B. ix, 8, 13, 29, 31, 37, 56, 57, 64, 72, 136, 140, 145, 146, 157

Churchman's 'The Design of Inquiring Systems' 136

clan 16

climate 51

closure 14, 132, 151

commodity xi, 48, 49

commodities of power 49, 161

communication 33, 35, 51, 52, 56, 110, 112, 129, 137, 139, 140, 142, 143

comparison vii, 10, 12, 22, 25-27, 29, 42, 51, 57, 61-64, 66, 73, 78, 95, 96, 98, 99, 105-113, 115-119, 121-123, 125-127, 131, 133, 134, 136, 150, 152, 155, 156, 162, 163

comparison
- exploratory 110, 111, 113, 116, 118, 119, 122, 126, 141
- diagnostic 111, 113, 117, 118, 121, 131
- design 111, 118, 121, 122, 125, 127

comparison chart 25

comparison process 12, 57, 61-63, 66, 78, 105-111, 125-127

components 67, 83, 93, 94, 103, 121

computers 1-3, 5-7, 140

conceptualization (law of) 64

conceptual model xi, 12, 23-25, 29, 35, 57, 59, 64, 66, 67, 69, 70, 84-87, 91-93, 95-97, 102, 104, 109, 116, 117, 122, 130, 131, 138, 149, 155, 156, 164

concern, area of, situation of 2, 3, 13, 14, 30, 74, 96, 145

conflict 18, 46, 51, 53, 54, 56, 64, 76, 138, 142, 143, 147
connectivity 93, 94, 103
consensus participation 143
consultative participation 141-143, 148
contingency 45
contingent 14, 16, 30, 31, 33, 43, 50, 52, 130, 159
control activities 89, 90, 100, 117
cultural analysis 17, 18, 42-46, 50, 133, 146
cultural beliefs 26
cultural values 19
culturally feasible 26, 79, 82, 97, 98, 100, 102, 108, 127, 128, 133, 150
culturally feasible changes 82, 97, 98, 100, 127
culturally infeasible 26
culture vii, 9, 16-18, 21, 26-28, 30, 39-46, 49, 51, 54, 128, 130, 145, 146, 150-153, 161
customer(s) 12, 22, 23, 53, 68, 71, 72, 74, 79, 83, 93

data 1, 2, 4-8, 112, 113, 116, 122, 123, 125, 131, 152
data analysis 6
debate 6, 12, 13, 26, 27, 29, 35, 37-39, 42, 43, 45, 47, 53, 54, 126-129, 131, 134, 136-139, 141, 143
decision taker 15, 16, 37-39, 148, 149, 151, 161
decision-making 36, 43, 47, 56, 93, 136
design 2, 3, 6, 25, 111, 118, 121, 122, 125, 127, 136, 140, 142
design phase 122
detailed comparison 122, 126
diagnosis 111, 113, 118, 121, 122
diagramming conventions xi
dialectical debate 38, 42
dialectical process 38, 136
dialectic(s) 37, 43, 136, 137, 139, 156
dialogical 110, 111, 112
dialogical comparison 112, 126

effectiveness 119-122

efficacy 119-122
efficiency 119-122
enquiry 1, 4, 15, 70, 103, 134, 158, 160, 162
entry 27, 103, 151, 155
environment 14, 23, 25-27, 62, 68, 71, 77, 78, 82, 93, 94, 103, 139
environmental constraints 12, 22, 23, 25, 71-73, 81, 90, 94
environmental element 71
ethics 50, 134, 140
ETHICS 140
ethnography 145, 146
exit 32, 33, 103, 151, 155
expert problem solver 35

Floppit Corporation 74-76, 79, 80, 82, 83, 97, 98, 100-102
formal system(s) model 25, 84, 92, 95, 102, 103
formal systems name 58, 63, 85
formalisms 45
framework viii, 1, 4, 6, 30, 34, 36, 39, 40, 43, 44, 47, 52, 59, 65, 75, 83, 86, 92, 93, 95, 103, 105, 107-110, 113, 117, 121, 125, 130, 131, 134, 136-138, 143, 144, 146, 150, 154, 158-163
framework of enquiry 103, 158, 160, 162

Galliers, R. 164
Geertz, C. 146
general systems theory 92
Goffmann's role theory 33

Hirschheim, R.A. 8, 164
history 27, 37, 40, 43, 45, 49, 123
how 113, 114
human activity system vii, 6, 12, 22, 26, 43, 55, 58, 59, 62, 63, 68, 69, 72, 79, 82, 84, 92, 93, 96-98, 100, 105, 109, 114, 125, 127, 129, 131, 138, 162, 164

ideal type vii, 10, 12, 13, 22, 137, 138, 149, 157, 162
ideological 110, 111, 112

ideological comparison approach 126

ill-formed, ill-structured 16, 31, 107

ill-understood 6

image 62, 69, 107, 109

impressions 12, 46, 130, 149, 154, 159

information vi, vii, viii, ix, 1-8, 10, 15-18, 20, 25, 28, 30, 52, 55, 64, 75, 81, 82, 89, 119, 123-126, 131, 132, 140, 142, 143, 146, 148, 152, 154-156, 158-164

information analysis 3, 4, 164

information management vi, vii, ix, 1, 3-8, 28, 140, 158-161, 163, 164

information manager 17, 55, 158-160

information requirements 3

information systems vi, viii, 8, 17, 140

information technology vii, 1, 5, 7, 15, 155

initiation 144, 151

initiator 15, 17, 26, 39, 148, 152, 153, 161

input xi, 19, 67-69, 72, 113, 124, 129

Inquiring system 136

intentionality 135

interpretation 2-4, 6-8, 16, 29, 30, 34, 110, 111, 116, 117, 119, 136, 146, 148, 150, 160

intervention vii, viii, 26, 135, 153

intuition 107

issue-based 58, 63, 64, 76-78, 83, 126

issue-based (non-service) 76, 77

issue-based (service) 76

issue-based system 63,64, 76-78, 83

IT strategy 15, 19, 21, 155

learning vi, vii, viii, ix, 1, 3-9, 12, 14-17, 22, 26, 27, 30, 38-40, 42-46, 53, 54, 57, 76, 82, 104, 107-109, 118, 126, 127, 131, 132, 134, 139, 141, 143, 148, 150, 151, 153, 154, 156, 158-164

learning environment 14

learning process vi, vii, viii, ix, 1, 3-7, 9, 27, 30, 38, 39, 42, 43, 53, 107, 108, 126, 132, 151, 156, 158-164

Liebenau, J. 1, 8

logical coherence 69

logical dependence 86, 88, 90, 94, 95, 98, 103, 123

Macdonald, W.B. 141, 157

Machiavellian 50

management vi, vii, viii, ix, 1-8, 20, 28, 30, 32, 41, 43, 53, 66, 76, 78, 79, 98, 112, 126, 127, 130, 135, 140, 142, 143, 156, 158-164

managing information vi, vii, viii, 1, 3, 6, 7, 10, 131, 156, 159, 160, 163

meaning 4, 6, 44, 45, 70, 159, 161

mental models 5

messy situations 16, 31

metaphor 10, 36, 53, 55, 143, 144, 148, 156

methodology vi, vii, viii, 6-17, 19, 22, 26-40, 42-44, 46, 47, 51-54, 56-60, 62, 63, 65-67, 73, 79, 82, 84-87, 92, 95, 97-100, 104-110, 116, 121, 125-141, 143-147, 149-158, 160-164

might-be relevant system 63

mind-set 42

mission 63, 92, 93, 103

mission statement 63

model overlay 112, 122-125

model-to-model 122

modelling language 86

modelling process 61, 74, 78, 84, 85, 91, 95, 96, 102, 105, 107, 109, 121, 131

models vii, 1, 5, 11-14, 22, 25-27, 35, 43, 45, 46, 51, 54, 57-64, 67, 69, 70, 71, 75, 79, 81, 82, 84, 85, 92, 93, 95-98, 100, 104, 107, 109-112, 117, 119, 122, 123, 126, 127, 131, 133, 134, 136, 138, 143, 150, 157, 162, 164

modes of comparison 111

Mumford, E. 140, 141, 145, 157

non-service system 63-65, 76, 77

norms 19, 40, 42, 45, 55, 130, 150, 161

observer 19, 93, 94

open system 60

operational activities 117

oppression 139

organization(al) 6-8, 15-18, 23-28, 31, 41, 44, 47, 49, 60-64, 76, 77, 81, 82, 97, 103, 119, 122-124, 127, 128, 141, 143, 14-155, 159, 160, 164

organizational change 49, 76

output xi, 2, 27, 67-69, 72, 105, 113, 114, 116, 117, 119, 120, 122, 124, 129

owner 12, 15, 16, 22, 23, 26, 33, 37-39, 53, 68, 70, 71, 73, 80, 81, 87, 90, 93, 94, 103, 129, 130, 148, 149, 161

participant observation 135

participant observer 19

participation 133, 140-143, 145, 147, 148, 157

participative process 35

performance 69, 71, 73, 93-95, 103, 119-122, 144

Plato 136

political analysis 18, 30, 46, 50

politics vii, 9, 16, 28, 46, 47, 49, 50, 54, 128, 161

power 37, 39, 42, 47-50, 70, 77, 93, 94, 103, 142, 148, 151, 161

power commodities 48-50

primary-task 58, 63, 64, 76-78, 83, 126

primary-task (non-service) 76, 77

primary-task (service) 76, 77

primary-task system 63, 64, 76-78, 83

problem content 30, 34, 35, 37, 77, 78

problem content system 77, 78

problem context 22, 39, 129

problem owner 15, 16, 26, 33, 37-39, 63, 64, 148, 149, 151, 161

problem situation vii, 9, 10, 12-18, 20-22, 25-30, 32-47, 49-51, 53, 54, 56, 58, 59, 84, 101, 103-105, 110-112, 126-129, 131, 133, 135, 138, 144, 146, 148-153, 155, 161, 162

problem solver 15, 19, 33-37, 39, 148, 149

problem solving 30, 34-37, 39, 76, 78, 79

problem solving system 30, 34-36, 39, 76, 78, 79

problems vi, vii, viii, 11, 14, 16, 17, 19, 27-32, 34, 36, 38, 41, 45, 61, 62, 64, 66, 75, 82, 105, 107, 109, 113, 117, 118, 121, 123, 124, 126, 131, 138, 141-143, 145-148, 150, 153, 161

process of management 126

purpose vi, 6, 14, 17, 36, 37, 52, 59, 60, 69, 92, 93, 103, 135, 136, 138, 139, 141, 144, 147, 153

purposeful human action 86

purposive model 12

rationality 136, 138, 139

real world vii, 10-15, 22, 25, 26, 31, 32, 37, 40, 42, 43, 54, 57, 59, 69, 74, 79, 96, 109, 110, 113, 114, 121, 125, 130, 135, 138, 149, 150, 154

reconstruction 159, 160

reflection viii, 1, 9, 14, 32, 47, 111, 132, 142, 144, 146, 148, 149, 158, 160, 163

regulatory function 93, 94, 103

relevance 11, 31, 43, 47, 54, 62, 64, 65

relevancy 22, 44, 46, 108, 110, 111, 113, 134

relevant vii, 2, 3, 12, 13, 16, 17, 21, 22, 25, 28-31, 35, 37, 43-45, 51, 53, 54, 57-59, 61-66, 69-72, 74-79, 81-83, 85, 96-98, 100, 104, 105, 109, 113, 116-118, 126, 130, 131, 134, 136, 148, 149, 150, 164

relevant system vii, 12, 13, 21, 22, 25, 28-30, 35, 51, 53, 54, 57-59, 61-66, 70-72, 74, 75-79, 81-83, 85, 96, 104, 105, 113, 116-118, 126, 130, 149, 150, 164

representative participation 142

resist change 42

resource 16, 18, 20, 23, 47, 53, 74, 76, 82, 87, 88, 94, 97, 98, 100-103

resources 16, 23, 28, 45, 53, 68, 71, 73, 81, 93-95, 103, 118-121, 128

rich picture xi, 20, 21, 27, 29, 46, 51, 56, 104, 130, 164

rigour 2, 95, 103, 126, 149

ritual 45

ritualistic 5, 17

role vii, 1, 5, 7, 9, 15, 16, 18, 19, 26, 28, 33-42, 45, 47, 50, 54, 55, 62, 70, 71, 107, 129, 130, 134, 140, 142, 148, 149, 151, 155, 158-160, 161, 164

role analysis 9, 15, 50, 54, 70

role-dependent 38, 40

role-expected 41

role related 40-42
role theory 33
root definition vii, 12, 22, 23, 25, 27, 57-59, 63, 64, 66-74, 78, 79, 81-87, 89-98, 100-105, 109, 110, 117, 118, 131, 149, 155, 156, 164
Rosenhead, J. 156

Scholes, J. 8, 13, 29, 37, 56, 57, 157
sense-making vi, vii, 6, 7, 34-36, 131, 158, 160-163
service 17, 18, 20, 58, 63-65, 76-78
service system 64, 65, 76, 78
similes 62
Singerian inquiring system 136
Sir Geoffrey Vickers 32
situation of concern 13, 14, 30
situations vii, viii, 6, 10-12, 16, 27, 28, 30, 31, 34, 40, 42, 47-52, 55-57, 59, 70, 96, 118, 126, 134, 135, 137, 143, 146, 148, 151, 154, 155, 156, 158, 160, 161
social changes 41
social construct(ion) 5, 31, 161
social reality vi, vii, 31, 35
social world vii, 5, 9, 16, 46, 57
socio-technical systems 140
soft systems methodology, SSM vi, vii, viii, 6-11, 13-15, 17, 19, 22, 26, 27, 29, 30, 31-34, 36, 38, 39, 42-44, 46, 50-54, 56-60, 62, 63, 65-68, 70, 72, 73, 78-82, 84-87, 89, 92-94, 97-100, 103, 104, 106-110, 116, 122, 123, 125, 127-131, 133, 135, 136, 139, 140, 143, 145, 147, 149, 151, 154-158, 160, 162, 163
software 1
solution 2, 3, 30, 33, 44, 76, 107
strategy 15-17, 19-21, 26, 27, 31, 145, 152, 153, 155
structured data collection 112, 113, 116, 122
structured questioning 113
subculture 46, 49
symbol 6
symbolic forms 41, 44, 45
symbols 43, 45
synthesis 136

system vii, 6, 12, 21-26, 30, 34-36, 39, 42, 51, 53, 55, 58-89, 92-98, 100, 101, 103, 104, 109, 111, 113, 114, 116-118, 121-125, 127, 128, 129, 131, 136-138, 149, 150, 155-157, 164
systemic 6, 11, 12, 35, 59, 60, 84
systemically desirable 79, 82, 97, 98, 100, 102, 108, 127, 133, 150
systems concepts 35, 43
systems models 11, 22, 46, 51, 57-59, 64, 75, 84, 96, 107, 109, 122, 138, 162
systems theory 60, 84, 92, 113
systems thinking 8-12, 22, 29, 42, 43, 54, 57, 59, 150, 158, 162

technology (as social construction) 5
thesis 136, 144
transformation 12, 22, 23, 68, 69, 71-74, 79, 88, 89, 98, 113
trap(s) 27, 30, 32, 33, 35, 36, 38-40, 44, 47, 50-52, 54, 56, 128, 134, 136, 137, 139, 149, 153, 159
typology of relevant systems 65, 66, 75

values 5, 17-19, 27, 31, 39-43, 45, 48-51, 53, 55, 69, 70, 73, 77, 107, 112, 130, 138, 147, 150, 161
Vickers, Sir G. 32, 40, 42, 56, 136, 137
viewpoint 50, 53, 137
viewpoints 39, 46, 53, 134, 136, 138, 140, 142, 161

Weltanschauung 12, 22, 23, 26, 68-71, 73, 80, 93, 112, 138, 145
what 113
wider system and environment 94, 103
Wilson, B. 8
work roles 41, 42, 148
world view vii, 12, 22, 134, 138, 139, 162, 52, 53, 55

zig-zag arrow xi